Northern General

R. L. Kell

Ian Allan
60th
ANNIVERSARY

Front cover:
October 1965, and Leyland Atlanteans outnumber all other traffic on the Tyne Bridge. No 1895, one of Northern's first batch of 1960, bodied by Metro-Cammell, heads for South Shields on trunk route 6. Behind, 1962 Roe 'flat-top' 2002 pulls into the bus stands on the bridge on service 12 to Ellen Wilkinson Estate on the edge of Gateshead. Gateshead & District No 108 (another Metro-Cammell) of 1963 is completing duty and will turn left off the Bridge for 'Foot of High Street'. In the far distance an early Alexander-bodied Atlantean of Newcastle Corporation works a joint service with Gateshead. *R. L. Kell*

Back cover:
Major Hayter's kipper boxes. Declining to buy heavyweight underfloor-engined chassis, Northern's General Manager bought time until the Tiger Cub and Reliance were marketed by turning to proven components and NGT design. Major Hayter and his design staff built an SOS-type 30ft straight-frame chassis, inserted AEC Regal running gear, and mounted a no-frills 43-seat body by Picktree of Chester-le-Street on top, and set the buses to work on the 2 and 10 Stanley–Newcastle services in 1953. All ended up at Stanley, where 1468/72/3 are seen in April 1961. Surrounding them are some of the excellent 1954 AEC Monocoach fleet. *R. L. Kell*

Contents

Further Reading

I have found the following books helpful and interesting on the operation of Northern and its subsidiaries. *From No Place to Success* by K. A. Jenkinson and S. A. Staddon (Autobus Review, 1995) is a detailed history. Full fleet details are given in the PSV Circle / Omnibus Society fleet histories PA4, PA6, PA13 and PA14. The Northern Group Enthusiasts' Club keeps up-to-date on fleet and services. The Limited Stop service is dealt with in *Tyne-Tees-Mersey* by K. Healey and P. Battersby (Venture Publications, 2000). Tramway operations are comprehensively described in *The Tramways of Gateshead* by G. S. Hearse (Author, 1965), *The Tramways of Sunderland* by S. A. Staddon (Advertiser Press, 1964) and *The Tramways of Northumberland* by G. S. Hearse (Author, 1961). *A History of British Bus Services — North East* by D. Holding (David & Charles, 1979) is a good guide to the area.

Title page:
Northern developed a practice of bringing older vehicles into the main fleet from the associated fleets, doubtless to concentrate experience and spare parts for dwindling models. Tynemouth's eight SE6 buses of 1935/6 were transferred in 1946. As prepared for Northern service as 1153, former Tynemouth T82 of 1935 with Short Bros body doesn't look like an 11-year-old machine. The sliding entrance door can be seen behind the grab-rail. In one window there is an anti-nationalisation poster promoting the BET-sponsored Omnibus Passengers' Protection Association. *Go North East*

First published 2002

ISBN 0 7110 2873 7

Published by Ian Allan Publishing

an imprint of Ian Allan Publishing Ltd, Hersham, Surrey KT12 4RG.

Printed by Ian Allan Printing Ltd, Hersham, Surrey KT12 4RG.

Code: 0209/B

Introduction

This book is a survey of the Northern General Transport Co Ltd and its associated companies and their operation of buses and coaches from 1913 under the ownership of the British Electric Traction Co Ltd until 1968.

Most of the Group companies developed from tramway operations which have been well recorded in a number of books, and only a brief scene-setting outline of tramway operations is given.

In this book it is not possible to give a full history of every vehicle, nor of every service, nor can the vehicles of operators taken into the Group business be considered in detail. Emphasis is given to the Company-ordered vehicle stock and, in particular, to developments which influenced the industry, for example Northern's own designed or modified vehicles, or those which raised the Company's profile nationally, such as the Routemaster purchase.

The Northern Group Associated Companies up to 1968 were:

- The Northern General Transport Co Ltd. Formed 1913, commenced operation 1914.
- The Gateshead & District Tramways Co, to Gateshead & District Omnibus Co 1950, to Gateshead & District Omnibus Co Ltd 1965.
- The Tynemouth & District Electric Traction Co Ltd, to Tynemouth & District Transport Co Ltd, 1934.
- The Jarrow & District Electric Traction Co Ltd. Ceased operations 1930.
- Wakefield's Motors Ltd, from LNER 1929.
- General County Omnibus Co Ltd, purchased 1930, ceased operating 1936.
- Sunderland District Omnibus Co Ltd from 1931.
- The Tyneside Tramways & Tramroads Co from 1936, to Tyneside Tramways & Tramroads Co Ltd 1965, to Tyneside Omnibus Co Ltd 1965.
- Bee-Line Continental Tours Ltd 1954-7.

The relatively modest quantity of literature devoted to the Group's operations is surprising, as it operated almost 1,000 buses and coaches in the 1950s, which was on a par with such major forces in the bus industry as United Automobile Services, Ribble and Crosville. The primary reason for this was, I believe, the relatively compact and industrial nature of the operating territory — the northern half of County Durham and the southeast corner of Northumberland, including much of the Tyneside conurbation. Relatively few outsiders travelled to the area who did not need to do so, and there were no major holiday resorts (even if Whitley Bay enjoyed popularity in the 1930s and 1950s, particularly with Scottish holidaymakers). The current vogue for exploring such magnificent cities as Newcastle-upon-Tyne and Durham was then unknown. The nearby countryside of Northumberland, North Yorkshire and western Durham was serviced by smaller bus operators or by United Automobile Services, whose operations surrounded the NGT Group. Only the superb touring coaches (of which the Northern General-designed SE6 six-wheelers of 1935 have a claim to be the best-ever touring coaches, for their time, designed and built in Britain) and the express services to the Lakes, Liverpool, Birmingham and Coventry gave a national presence to the Group's confined operations.

So why does the Northern Group deserve more than the passing attention devoted to a British Electric Traction area company? Firstly, it had a very strong engineering direction, which exercised considerable influence upon the PSV manufacturing and operating industry. While most in evidence in the work of Major (later Colonel) G. W. Hayter (until 1955), this continued with various fleet engineers until recent times and the closure of Bensham Works. Secondly, there was a magnificent coaching fleet maintained and operated by selected staff. Thirdly, it introduced innovative express services, initially as a fast operation running parallel with existing inter-urban bus services. Finally, for the enthusiast, there was the individual character of the associated fleets in various liveries, some with standard Group-specification vehicles, and some with individual specifications. Frequent inter-company vehicle transfers added to the spice, such as a Northern wartime Guy Arab in Gateshead chocolate livery working for Sunderland District.

I should like to acknowledge and thank many for their generosity of time and assistance, which has been essential to the production of the book. Chris Moyes, Deputy Managing Director of Go-Ahead Group PLC, and David Slater of Go North East have made Company records available. Many staff and ex-staff have shared their memories and opinions. The enthusiast organisations of the PSV Circle, the Omnibus Society (particularly the Northern Branch) and the Northern Group Enthusiasts' Club and their members have contributed enormously. Staff of Beamish, the North of England Open Air Museum, Durham County Records Office, Tyne & Wear Archives Service, the Universities of Durham and Warwick and the Birmingham & Midland Motor Omnibus Trust have been equally helpful.

Friends who have assisted include Bob Davis, Roy Marshall, David Wayman, Geoff Burrows, Alan Hedley, Ted Heslop, Ian Findlay, Trevor Hines, Graham Dudley, Chris Redpath, Arthur Staddon, John Watson, Derek High, Philip Battersby, Robert Atkinson, Brian Smith, Peter Kell, George Nairn, Ray Thornton, David Little, Gordon Turner, Arnold Richardson and many more. Memories and conversations past still come to mind from the late Bill Barnes, Joe Gardner, Colin Ritchie, Roland Dixon, Douglas Inch, Peter Hardy and Tom Steele.

I hope that the reader will experience some of the pleasure that the Group gave to me in travel on its outstandingly reliable services throughout the North East on many fascinating and innovative vehicles.

R. L. Kell
Durham, May 2002

The British Electric Traction Co (BET) was formed in London in 1896 to promote and co-ordinate electric traction in Britain and abroad. It purchased existing tramway companies and developed wider transport interests as tramways were replaced by bus operations, setting up the British Automobile Traction Co (BAT) to develop the motor transport operations. The British Electrical Federation Ltd (BEF) acted as designer, adviser and purchasing contractor for vehicles etc for Federation companies. BET operators used the insignia of a winged wheel within a magnet on vehicles and uniforms.

Tramways in Gateshead

In 1897 BET acquired the **Gateshead & District Tramways Co** as one of its first major purchases. The Gateshead & District Tramways Act of 1889 had allowed the construction of street tramways but it was 1893 before rails were laid and double-deck tramcars were hauled by steam tram locomotives. This must have been a spectacular form of transport, but BET gained extensions to and electrification of the system, and electric trams started in 1901. The system was completed in 1903 to Wrekenton (a climb

The start of it all. Gateshead Tramways Straker-Squire CO model, J 2119, with Birch 28-seat body, photographed in London for the coachbuilder in 1913. This bus went into the Northern fleet in 1914 but was requisitioned in September and converted into an Army lorry. It did not return to Northern. Unlike the double-deckers, the bus had a windscreen.
R. L. Kell collection

to the southeast) and to the important terminus at Low Fell (on the Great North Road to the south). The livery of the trams was chocolate brown (termed maroon by the company) and white, and the depot was in Sunderland Road, its extensive facilities including bodybuilding. Until 1923 the tramways of Gateshead and Newcastle were separated by the River Tyne. Travellers had to alight at each end of Stephenson's High Level Bridge and pay a halfpenny toll to walk over or ride on Howe's 'ha'penny lop' horse bus for the same price, the operator paying fourpence toll to the North Eastern Railway for a 40-seat bus. The company also started a Tramway Parcels Express (TPE) delivery service in 1905 with horse-drawn carts, which was converted to motor vans (latterly Commers) over a 20-mile radius from the tram depot.

Powers to run omnibuses had been gained by Gateshead & District Tramways in 1909. Chester-le-Street Urban District Council requested bus services in its area, and in 1912 the company built a bus garage for 30 buses and workshops in Picktree Lane, Chester-le-Street. This was to become the centre of Gateshead motor-bus operations. Buses were ordered in preparation for the start of the first service on 7 May 1913 from Low Fell tram terminus to Chester-le-Street. Waiting rooms were provided on Kell's Lane Corner, Low Fell, for passengers changing between bus and tram.

Daimler bus chassis were the first choice, but with their limited availability, the first vehicles to be delivered were Sidney Straker & Squire Ltd 29hp CO models supplied in 1913 by BAT. Eight buses (and one lorry) were supplied, each costing £528 13s 6d for the chassis and £135 per body. Four were Birch-bodied single-deckers on longer chassis and four were double-deckers; all seated 34. Another two Strakers may have followed. All were said to comply with the requirements of the London Police Authority in terms of weight, silence (!) and mobility. Daimler CC 40hp double-deckers (at £565 each) arrived later in 1913, three batches of five being followed by partial delivery of further batches, some single-deck. The double-deckers were fitted with second-hand bodies from the (London) Metropolitan Steam Omnibus Co and the London General Omnibus Co, at £78 each. A number of experienced drivers accompanied these vehicles north and remained with the company.

As buses were delivered, further services were started, some requested by local authorities and most radiating from the Chester-le-Street garage. The Low Fell service proved immensely popular and alone required nine buses.

The 'Gateshead Tramways Motor Service' buses were painted ▲ in the tramcar livery. In October 1913 R. W. Cramp was appointed to manage the operations of the motor-bus fleet (or 'Motor Department', as it was then known), W. F. Endean taking over at Gateshead.

Other BET tramways on Tyneside

As well as the Gateshead operation, BET owned two other tramways on Tyneside. The North Shields & Tynemouth District Tramways Ltd was bought in 1899. Formerly horse-, then steam-operated, it was renamed by BET as the **Tynemouth & District Electric Traction Co Ltd** and the gauge increased from 3ft to 3ft 6in. Through-running to Newcastle over the lines of the independent Tyneside Tramways system was not possible. Electric operations started in 1901 over a single line from North Shields to Whitley Bay with double-deck tramcars in crimson lake and cream. Depots were at Suez Street, North Shields, and John Street, Cullercoats. Buses replaced the trams in August 1931.

The **Jarrow & District Electric Traction Co Ltd** was a small tramway with a prolonged conception, BET taking an interest in 1903. Protracted negotiations with Jarrow and South Shields

Pre-World War 1 days in Chester-le-Street. The Gateshead Tramways Straker-Squire double-decker, J 2117, is the only motor vehicle on the Great North Road in 1913. It wasn't to last long, as it was requisitioned in 1914. The body is probably a 32-seater by Immisch, which was sold to Aldershot & District. The location is almost identical to that showing NGT 1805 on page 68, but the Co-op store was rebuilt following a fire in 1933. *G. Nairn*

►

Chester-le-Street depot, 1913. The first garage for buses was built by Gateshead Tramways in Picktree Lane, which runs to the front of the depot bays in this view. Much enlarged, it is still used by Go-Ahead Northern. *R. L. Kell collection*

corporations led to the birth of the electric system in November 1906, and through-running over the South Shields system was arranged from June 1908. Three years later, arguments with South Shields (no pushover in transport matters) left the sickly infant as a rump, with transfer to the Corporation trams at Tyne Dock. The Board of Trade would not permit the system to extend westwards to meet the Gateshead trams because this would involve crossing rope-worked coal-carrying railways, and thus ended plans for a South Tyneside linear tramway. Joint operation with South Shields resumed in 1922, but the 10 double-deck maroon-and-off-white trams were suffering from bus competition, and the system closed in June 1929. Northern SOS Q buses, with 'JARROW' fleetnames, covered the service (J) for a year until the licences were transferred to Northern. The small, forgotten Jarrow company ceased trading but was not formally wound up until 1948. The corrugated-iron depot in Swinburne Street was used for storage until it was demolished in 1946.

The founding of Northern General

With the initial success of the Low Fell–Chester-le-Street buses, BET formed a holding company to co-ordinate its motor-bus services in the North East, and this was registered on 29 November 1913 as the **Northern General Transport Co Ltd**. Shareholders in the tramway companies were offered shares in the new company, and the former tramway companies became constituents (or associated companies) of the NGT. The use of the word 'General' in the title allowed the company to carry out other transport activities such as the supply and hire of vehicles, the carriage of parcels and goods and the operation of Royal Mail contracts. A reason for setting up the Northern company was the inflexible nature of the statutory Gateshead Tramways Co, which would have had to seek Parliamentary powers for any new activities.

Northern General started operations on 1 January 1914, when the Company purchased the buses and garage of Gateshead Tramways. Northern acquired 26 buses, and a further 24 were ordered. Over one million passengers had been carried by the Gateshead buses and 300,000 miles run. The services inherited from Gateshead Tramways ran from Chester-le-Street to Low Fell and Durham, and to Craghead, Edmondsley and Fence Houses, from Heworth tram terminus to Washington and from Dunston tram terminus to Scotswood.

Northern General and the war years

With Northern General now established at its Chester-le-Street garage (which was extended to accommodate 50 buses) and the 24 or so Daimler B and CD buses ordered by Gateshead Tramways now being delivered, rapid expansion of services continued in 1914.

A fleet colour of all-red was adopted for the new and repainted Tramways fleet, with a large underlined 'NORTHERN' fleetname in gold on the side panels. Some vehicles were lined out in gold. Vehicles were still identified by their chassis number, which was clearly painted on the bonnet side or exposed chassis side. The fleet continued to be registered in County Durham with J 2xxx registrations but was subject to much rebodying and re-chassising, so the numbers were carried, in some cases, by more than one 'vehicle'.

The new 1914 services, operated with 10 new single-deckers, ran from Chester-le-Street to Stanley and Consett, from Newcastle to Consett and to Stanley, and from Sunderland to Heworth tram terminus (quickly closed, due to poor receipts). Tynemouth Tramways also started a service north of the Tyne, from North Shields to Seaton Delaval and Whitley Bay.

This rapid development, particularly in the west of the county in the Stanley and Consett areas far from tramway operation, meant that further operational bases were needed. The first of these, in Stanley, was a converted skating rink opened in August 1914 and allowed Newcastle services to start. Stanley was (and still is) one of the main centres of Northern operations and, with its higher elevation, presented more severe winter climate and gradient challenges than the rest of the system. The services out of Heworth are believed to have operated out of the Jarrow Tramways depot.

The high point of development had now been reached, for in August 1914 war was declared. This had a major impact upon the Company's existing system and plans, for three main reasons. Firstly, vehicles were needed by the Army for transporting men and materials, both in Britain and in France and Belgium. Secondly, the numbers of men who volunteered or were conscripted into the Armed Services (particularly of experienced drivers, who were in great demand) reduced staff availability, and this led to higher wage rates for continuing staff. Thirdly, there was a lack of trade and workmen to travel in some areas, due notably to short-time working in the Stanley-area collieries. To these may be added a fourth — the deteriorating condition of roads, which were now subject to

heavy motor traffic but had fewer staff to repair them; again, the Stanley and Annfield Plain areas appear to have suffered particularly. ▲

The Northern fleet of 54 in August 1914 was more than halved to 26, and the carriage of nearly three million passengers a year would not be exceeded until 1919. Half the services were temporarily withdrawn, leaving the core services (Durham–Low Fell, Chester-le-Street–Stanley, Stanley–Newcastle) plus intermittent operation of some others. Withdrawal of the North Shields service would have long-term consequences, allowing United Automobile Services (running from Blyth in Northumberland) to colonise some of the south Northumberland services before Tynemouth Tramways started its bus services in 1921.

The Straker-Squire chassis, only a year or so old, were early departures and were driven to Aldershot (or the manufacturer's); the bodies were sold. Fourteen Daimlers were sent via BAT on hire to Aldershot & District. They did not return, being distributed to other BET companies and re-registered in the LP 8xxx series. Further Daimlers, purchased under the Government 'subsidy' scheme whereby operators had cheaper chassis which could be called up by the authorities, were impressed as lorries. Many of the J registrations would, however, be reused for new buses postwar.

The war years of 1914 to 1918 imposed considerable strains on the depleted staff and fleet. Extra demands arose to support the Military and to cater for the settlement of 20,000 Belgian refugees at Elisabethville, Birtley, increasing traffic on the Low Fell–Chester-le-Street service. Munitions factories also opened in the

This picture is believed to have been taken at Chester-le-Street in late 1914 as bus chassis were being prepared for the War Department. There are four Daimler chassis, CC 568, 559, 542 and 244 (from the right). These would have been buses J 2543, J 2338, J 2337 and J 2502, all of 1913.
The Straker-Squire on the far left is less easy to identify. It appears to have bonnet (chassis) number CO961A or 964A, and as such was probably a chassis built up by Northern from spare parts. The WD bodies were presumably built by NGT.
Go North East

Birtley area. Women were employed as conductresses for the duration of the war, and the shortage of drivers was met by training pitmen to drive part-time, some of whom eventually joined full-time Northern staff.

Various fuels were tried to reduce reliance on imported petrol. Paraffin oil and other spirits were used, and a coal-gas filling station was installed at Chester-le-Street. Large bags tied down to wooden framing around the top of single-deckers provided the fuel store. The Company regarded such experiments as relatively successful, and the experience gained would prove useful in the 1930s.

A further strain on the Company's resources was competition from motor cars such as Model T Fords ('jitneys'), fitted with capacious (if sometimes ramshackle) bodies, whose owners attempted to 'cream off' passengers from the hard-pressed services, particularly to Newcastle. Northern responded with the introduction of seven General Motors Model 15 light buses in 1916/17 but their lives were short and all were gone by the end of 1919, some to serve as Gateshead parcel vans and depot lorries. Although more Daimler buses on order were requisitioned at the factory, some of the single-deck bodies ordered were taken into stock and used to rebody existing double-deckers.

As part of Northern's 'General' transport activities, contracts from the GPO were obtained in 1915 to

carry mails in the Newcastle, Sunderland and Haswell areas. A Tilling-Stevens van, J 3350, was obtained, but difficulties later arose and the mail contracts were given up. In addition, Northern also advertised the availability of hire and maintenance of vans from its Chester-le-Street depot in 1914.

Expansion with Daimlers, 1919-25

The Armistice in November 1918 allowed the Company to restart expansion plans as new and ex-Army commercial chassis became available. The return of surviving troops gave NGT opportunities but also a potential threat. Many soldiers had been trained in driving and in vehicle maintenance, and knowledgeable staff thus became available locally. The threat was that these individuals, supplemented by miners who had made some savings or could buy vehicles on hire-purchase, would turn to the individual provision of transport for both goods and people.

Orders for new bus chassis were placed by Northern in 1919 for 40 Leylands and then 50 AECs. With long delivery times, only six of the Leylands came into service, and these were sold and the remainder cancelled. The majority of the AECs were also cancelled, but five were retained as they were quite similar to the Daimler Y-type. Standardisation on Daimler chassis, mainly Y-types, continued until 1925. Ten Daimlers arrived in 1919, 37 in 1920, 29 in 1921, 11 in 1922 and nine in 1923. In addition there were five ex-War Department Royal Air Force tenders on Crossley pneumatic-tyred chassis which were fitted out as 14-seat buses and charabancs.

The fleet was increasing fast, from 49 in 1919 to 75 at the end of 1920 and 95 by the end of 1921. This allowed the Company to reintroduce the services suspended in 1914/15, increase the frequency of existing services and introduce new ones. This included the use of Bewick Street (opposite the Central station) in Newcastle as a terminus for routes operating from the Stanley area across the Redheugh Bridge (and paying the tolls!).

In 1919 Northern commenced a series of vehicle bonnet numbers prefixed by a chassis-identification letter, which replaced the use of prominent chassis numbers. The short series were AEC chassis (AEC1-5), Crossley (C1-5), General Motors (GMC1-5) and Leyland (L1-6). The main sequence was, of course,

Daimler, which ran initially from D1 to D80 but thereafter continued until the end of 1926, when D306 was reached. This numerical sequence included some 'S' numbers (for SOS S types, but which were not carried). The last flowering of the 'D' series came with the use of D373-82 for 10 Associated Daimlers in 1928. Early Tynemouth vehicles retained their Northern numbers.

A new bus livery was also adopted postwar. This was Northern BET red for panels, bonnet and wheels with gold lining-out. Chassis, panel beadings and mudguards were picked out in black. The window-surrounds and roof were white, with a cantrail line above the windows in black on some vehicles. The large, underlined fleetname and bonnet numbers were gold. The associated Tynemouth Tramways/Tynemouth & District livery was identical apart from the fleetname. 'TYNEMOUTH TRAMWAYS' was used initially, but 'TRAMWAYS' was later dropped. However, 'COAST LINE SERVICE' was added to Tynemouth single-deckers after the opening of the new coast road to Tynemouth in 1928.

Vehicles of this period, while having surprisingly long lives, required frequent maintenance, and the bodies also took a

The first fleet-numbered bus was Daimler B type J 2551 of 1914. The picture shows it in its rebuilt 1919 condition in the new red-and-white livery. Body changes were frequent with these early buses, D1 being, at various times, a double-decker, a single-decker and a lorry. This body is probably either a Birch or Northern-rebuilt Birch one. The bus went to Tynemouth & District Electric Traction in 1921 as its No 1.
Beamish North of England Open Air Museum

Northern bought some ex-Royal Air Force Crossley tenders in 1920 for use as small 14-seat buses to combat competition. The body on C2 could be described as a 'lorry-bus', being a conversion of the original tender body. It certainly isn't the new Ransomes body which was fitted later. These little Crossleys had a reasonable and intensive life of six or so years with Northern.
Go North East

By 1921 body design was settling on the BEF specifications used throughout the BET Group. Brush of Loughborough was the principal supplier of BEF bodies, and these rear-entrance Daimler Ys are ready to be driven north. This batch (D84-7) survived intact until the late 1920s and were not involved in rebuilding into Long Ys. *Go North East*

▲ pounding from poor roads in mining areas. Consequently increased workshop space was required to overhaul chassis and bodies separately. Land was purchased at Queen Street, Gateshead, and new overhaul workshops, running depot and administrative buildings were constructed in 1920/1. These essentially replaced Chester-le-Street workshops, allowing the operational depot there to be enlarged. The following year Major G. W. Hayter, then a young ex-Army engineer, was appointed as Chief Engineer. A new era was dawning.

While Daimlers were the chassis of choice and many were purchased through BAT, body suppliers were more varied. Brush, Dodson and Birch, Latymer and Ransomes all supplied buses of various styles to Northern, often via BAT. Early bodies (up to 1921), both single- and double-deck, had rear entrances, sometimes supplemented by up-front seats beside the driver. As the conductor could not easily reach these seats, fare money could be given to the driver, and this became known as 'driver's perquisites' (or 'perks', in modern parlance). From 1922, however, a change was made to forward-entrance single-deckers, and BEF-specification drawings were the basis of designs used by many of the BET bus operators. Thereafter NGT was wedded to the forward entrance, and no further Northern single-deckers were rear-entrance.

Gordon Hayter's appointment in the spring of 1922 was to prove an influential one, initially for NGT and later for the industry as a whole. With new workshops at Bensham under his control already overhauling and reconstructing chassis and bodies, he was in a strong position to design and develop a range of standard vehicles based upon the wartime Daimler Y-type and rationalise the various body styles. Hayter was a strong character with frequently expressed opinions as well as a good engineer, and this attracted the press. The oft-repeated story quoted by S. Walls of *Bus and Coach* magazine in an interview with Major Hayter in September 1946 is that the Chief Engineer went to Slough in 1924 and bought 100 old Y-type Daimlers which he fitted with steel bodies and that this fleet was the foundation of the business. From 1919 NGT had been buying ex-War Department Daimler/AEC chassis from the Slough Trading Co (which handled Army sales) as well as from BAT, which acted as a clearing-house for sale and transfer of surplus chassis or bodies. From 1922 to 1925 around 63 ex-Slough chassis entered service, of which 45 were directly ex-WD. There may well have been others used for spare parts, but Northern's own stock of over 100 Daimlers (at the end of 1921) was available for recycling. Twenty further Daimlers came into the fleet from the purchase of two independent operators. Most of these were Daimler 'heavyweight' models B, CC, CD, W and Y. A few were medium-weight,

20-seat models CB, CJ and CK (or CJK). Gordon Hayter quickly appreciated that the heavyweights were, in fact, unnecessarily heavy, but he wasn't alone in that. Even more important figures in the industry were thinking along similar lines in the early 1920s.

The postwar period saw Northern change from a tramway-feeder operation (principally to the Gateshead Tramways at Low Fell in the south, Dunston in the southwest and Heworth in the southeast) to a genuinely co-ordinated network. In the 1920-2 period, services were introduced from Newcastle to Blaydon, to Stanley via Tantobie and Annfield Plain and to Consett via Sunnyside, and from Sunderland to Durham, to South Shields and to Chester-le-Street, as well as local services in the Stanley and Consett areas.

A major development was the transfer of five Daimler B-types (three as double-deckers but to be converted to single-deckers) to Tyneside Tramways in July 1921 to start a service from North Shields to Whitley Bay and Blyth on the Northumberland coast; this was to defend the Tynemouth & District tramway against attack by United Automobile Services, which ran competing buses from its Blyth garage. This area was to become a running sore between the two companies for years, despite agreements between Northern and United concerning non-competition in their respective 'areas' in County Durham — 'area' agreements. It also marked the start of Northern/Tynemouth inter-fleet transfers which were numerous and regular over many years. Some of these were recorded formally by numbering the bus into the new operational fleet. A vehicle going back into its 'original' fleet was given a new fleet number rather than resuming its original one, and in this way a bus gained a variety of fleet numbers as it travelled around the Group companies. Many vehicles worked temporarily or 'on hire' to another Group company, and some of these were not recorded. Henceforward the Northern and Tynemouth fleets will be treated together, as they shared fleet orders for much of the period.

The expansion and consequent in-filling with shorter services led to an increased demand for local garages to supplement Chester-le-Street and Stanley. The running (service) depot at Bensham, Gateshead, opened in 1924, as did premises in Holmeside, Sunderland. Chester-le-Street gained a major extension, and the first phase of a new depot at Consett opened — all in a single year!

Northern's first acquisition of a rival concern occurred when Isaac Walton's Crescent Bus Co of Gateshead was purchased in January 1924. Walton had competed with Northern on the Gateshead–Durham service, which had been extended from Low Fell tram terminus to a stand near the Gateshead High Level Bridge in February 1921. Most of Walton's fleet were Daimlers, and these fitted in with Northern's own stock. Land from Walton near the High Level Bridge was used to build a bus station at Wellington Street, which opened in 1925 and, although a backwater once the new Tyne Bridge opened, served as a terminus for Tynemouth's cross-Tyne service.

The second purchase, in April 1925, was that of Hall Bros 'Invincible Motor Omnibus Company' with services south from Sunderland to the Seaham Harbour, Dawdon and Murton areas near the East Coast. This took Northern into new operating areas, and the Hall Bros premises were used for a year or two. Again, Daimlers were the mainstay of the fleet and were taken into stock.

The rebuilding of Daimler Ys into longer standard 38-seaters (including aisle seats) commenced in 1923 and continued as fast as Bensham could turn them out. This is the 'Big Bertha', including all the improvements that Major Hayter, Chief Engineer, could muster — the 'inside-out' chassis can be seen at the front. The Knight-patent sleeve-valve Daimler engine was retained, as Northern had sorted out the 'oil-burner', and it provided smooth, quiet (if not particularly quick) travel. Gordon Hayter said of them: 'The more they knocked, the better they went'. No D160 was nominally an AEC YC (AEC1 of 1919) but was now 'Daimlerised' and fitted with this Brush front-entrance (now standard) body. After conversion to pneumatics it lasted until 1934. Trade plate 0017 J is still used by Go North East today. *Go North East*

As well as big Daimlers, Northern built up a fleet of smaller C types, still with the sleeve-valve engine. No D129 was from the 1924 purchase of Isaac Walton's 'Crescent' fleet and was registered X 8686 in 1920. Walton's built the 20-seat body and converted it to (massive) pneumatic tyres. It is seen in Durham Market Place awaiting return to Sunderland; the date must be 1924, as the bus was withdrawn that year to be 'Northernised' into the first NGT-Daimler Long CB, and as such would be one of the last Daimlers to run for Northern, in 1935. It would also be converted to run on town gas (with compressed-gas cylinders) for a time in 1932. *G. Nairn*

The final flowering of the rebuilt Daimlers were the LYs of 1925/6. No D285 was probably one of the BEF-inspired 'lightweight' buses of the period, as a parallel design to BMMO's S type. The Brush body was a 31-seater. The chassis did not have a long life, being replaced by an SOS in 1930. The livery is Northern red and white, with black wings and mouldings and gold lining-out on the red. The radiator is very like that of the S type but with an additional bulge on top. *Go North East*

During the early 'Twenties the motley fleet of solid-tyred Daimlers met increasing predation of Northern's regular timed services by the owners of 'jitneys' and small buses which creamed off traffic at busy times. The availability of ex-World War 1 commercial chassis, old limousine cars and, increasingly, lightweight and fast American and Italian chassis posed a serious threat, particularly when private owners grouped together to run timetabled services in what Northern saw as its own backyard. In 1922 six ex-WD Daimler CBs fitted with new Ransomes 20-seat forward-entrance bodies and pneumatic tyres, together with six pneumatic-tyred Crossley 14-seaters, formed a small defensive fleet to counter this competition.

From 1923 the large fleet of Daimler Y/AEC YC models were progressively taken into Bensham Works, and, effectively, turned into new buses by Gordon Hayter and his staff. New lightweight pressed-steel chassis frames were built to a longer 16ft 3in wheelbase, some replacing wood/steel 'flitch' originals. Unusually frames were used 'inside-out', with the U-pressing facing outwards rather than inward as per conventional automobile practice. Ball races replaced plain bushes in the wheel hubs. The Knight patent sleeve-valve Daimler engine was adopted as standard and was fitted to rebuilt AECs. The buses were fitted with 38-seat steel-framed bodies to a standard BAT/BEF design by Brush, Ransomes or Vickers and, known as 'Big Berthas', became Northern's standard until 1926. The 38 seats, however, included gangway tip-up seats together with a 'suicide' seat mounted on the rear emergency door, lifting upwards when the door mechanism was opened. The extra seats were later removed and the buses reverted to normal 31- or 32-seaters.

Some rebuilds of old Northern stock were given new NGT-Daimler chassis numbers in a series 1 to 63. In 1925 there was a further series of Northern-rebuilt Y-types in a 'Long Y' sequence (LY1-24). However, the seating capacity of all pre-1930 Road Traffic Act buses remains a variable quantity, given Gordon Hayter's wish to maximise seating capacity.

Originally on solid tyres, the early 'Big Berthas' were converted to pneumatic tyres from 1927 to 1929. However, the LYs of 1925/6 and LCBs of 1926 were constructed from new with pneumatic tyres and steel disc wheels.

In line with developments elsewhere in the industry, attempts were made by BET/BEF in the mid-1920s to lighten the full-size bus. Gordon Hayter refers to 'one of a number of BEF lightweight buses' in the context of a Ransomes rebody of a Daimler chassis rebuilt by Northern. The identity of this experimental bus is not clearly established but may have been D265, serving as the prototype for the final Daimler rebuilds of 1926, the lengthened CB chassis LCB1-5. No doubt lightweights compared with the Y-type rebuilds, they were fitted with (light) BMMO-design bodies as fitted to the SOS 'S' type. These were the last chassis constructed at Bensham for seven years and survived until the end of the Daimler sleeve-valve era in 1935. The works had turned out at least 98 'new' standard buses, along with many others reconstructed and rebodied. Despite Northern's attempts to lighten and update the sleeve-valve Daimler, events elsewhere were passing it by.

2. Save Our Services — Enter the SOS, 1924

In the search for lighter, faster and more reliable full-size buses than the major chassis builders could provide, the lead was taken by the Chief Engineer of the Birmingham & Midland Motor Omnibus Co Ltd, L. G. Wyndham Shire. Taking the contemporary Tilling-Stevens TS3 chassis (which BMMO ran in quantity) and re-working it to lighten it and to improve durability and reliability in service, and also designing light but strong jig-built wooden bodies using experience gained in aircraft construction in World War 1, established the foundation of a good and lively bus operating on pneumatic tyres. When the Tilling 4.3-litre four-cylinder engine was lightened with a Ricardo alloy cylinder head and pistons and higher compression ratio to improve efficiency and raise operating speed, a masterpiece, the BMMO/SOS 'S' (or Standard), was offered for trial by BMMO to other BET operators, and Northern ordered one in 1924 — No D168 (registered PT 3422

as a Tilling-Stevens) with Brush/BMMO-design 32-seat body. Light, fast, reliable and capable of being driven enthusiastically, this was the bus to tackle developing competition. Northern General and Gordon Hayter were impressed and ordered 50 of the new machines — Northern's largest single bus order to date (later matched by Routemasters). The buses arrived in 1925 (fleet numbers 207-56), followed by a further 10 (292-301) and six for Tynemouth (6-11) in 1926.

The 1930/1 rolling-stock programme approved the reconstruction of 61 SOS buses at £250 each. Later axles and smaller wheels were fitted and the bodywork was lowered. Withdrawals of S types started in 1935, but a few lingered on into the war period and saw nearly 20 years of service. One notable use after service was that of No 233 (PT 4917); withdrawn in 1936, it was bought for use as a transport and baggage van for the 1936 Jarrow March of the unemployed to London — Jarrow to London in bottom gear!

Two ex-BMMO S charas were reconstructed on longer frames with new Short Bros 36-seat (but still normal-control) bodies. Nos 587 (HA 2437) and 592 (HA 2440) would thus have had long lives, originally on service and later as driver-trainers, 587 at Chester-le-Street and 592 at Bensham; 587 thus saw 30 years of service, being one of the last SOSs to be withdrawn in 1955 and by then one of the oldest PSVs in use in the country. Publicity for this was then seen as complimentary; now it would be taken as condemnatory!

In 1926 BMMO developed the S into a forward-control maximum-capacity (37 seats) single-decker, the Q (Queen), which was still very light at 4 tons 4cwt. Twenty-five were 'reserved' with BMMO in September 1926 at £1,330 each (Nos 307-31). Tynemouth also took 11 (T12/4-23). The Qs, still with two-wheel brakes, had long lives, most surviving 19 or 20 years, some as ambulances for Civil Defence during the 1939-45 war. Happily one still survives, Northern 321 (CN 2870), which Ted Heslop of Hexham rescued from a caravan site (the fate of many Qs) and passed on to the Birmingham & Midland Motor Omnibus Trust at Wythall, near Birmingham, where restoration has now restarted on Northern General's oldest surviving bus.

The year 1928 brought the entry of what was to prove one of the great bus designs of all time, the QL (Queen Low). Taking the Q mechanics, fitting smaller wheels (twin at the rear), reducing the rear axle ratio to improve hill-climbing and upgrading to four-wheel brakes gave the driver (who had an enamel warning notice about the brakes in the cab) a lively vehicle that was better than most in 1928. The 37-seat body (Northern licensed many as 40-seaters originally) was very similar to that of the Q.

Northern took 65 QLs in 1928, the most ever of one model in a single year, with five more going to Tynemouth. Later a further 11 examples were acquired second-hand from Trent. This massive intake meant that the QL was seen everywhere on the system and cleared out most of the unmodernised Daimlers. Its performance had a lasting effect on the senior staff of Northern which was to resurface 25 years later. On the road the QL presented a pugnacious and business-like presence, particularly when the bodies were rebuilt with 'loft-conversion' roller-blind destination indicators in the roof to replace wooden boards. Its major (and by far its most competent) competitor in the 1920s bus wars was the Leyland Lion PLSC of 1926/7, run by Sunderland District and ABC of Consett.

Ten QLC coaches (363-70/83/4) introduced to the fleet a new coachbuilder, Short Bros of Rochester, Kent. The Short brothers had a strong North East connection — their father had been an engineer in the Durham coalmines —and had built up one of the major early aeroplane-manufacturing companies, turning to coachbuilding in the 1920s following the cessation of World War 1 aircraft production. The company was to become Northern's 'house' coachbuilder, producing specialised designs as well as BMMO/BEF-designed bodies until rising political tension in Europe led to concentration on aircraft, particularly seaplanes, at Rochester under the grand title 'Short Bros (1928) Rochester & Bedford Ltd', at Seaplane Works, Rochester, Kent.

Although it was reliable and lively, passenger comfort was not the QL's strongest point, and the lack of entrance doors was remedied in 1931. Surprisingly, in view of their long lives (most serving 20 to 22 years), there was no modernisation of the body structure, and the whole fleet retained the comparatively high

Early SOS buses were uncompromising, idiosyncratic and endearing. Northern's first half-cab bus was the Q (or Queen). To accommodate the cab beside the engine, the engine and driveline has been moved to the nearside to allow the driver, who sat on the petrol tank, some (but not much) room. No 328 carries a Northern-fitted stencil-box for service numbers, prefixed by 'N'; route boards would be carried along the side or in a slot across the front nearside window. This photograph dates from 1931/2, when the Qs were modernised with single-curved panelling over the angular rockers, but the front is little changed apart from helmet wings replacing the original cycle type. The 1927 Qs, unlike the later QLs, were not fitted with rooftop destination-blind boxes. Note Northern's unusual lighting arrangements — large sidelamps and low-mounted driving lamps — which persisted until World War 2. Folding doors have now been fitted at the top of the steps, to keep out those cold winds. The 37-seat Q was fitted with single rear wheels.
Go North East

15

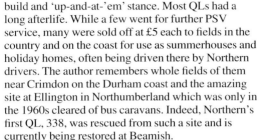

The SOS QL was a lower-geared, four-wheel-braked development of the Q — a go-anywhere, do-anything bus. The Company loved them, and drivers indulged in a very sporting performance which could see off most of the opposition in 1928. The scene is at East Stanley, just outside the Northern garage, with the Territorial Drill Hall in the background. The photograph is dated 4 August 1939 — a month before war was declared with Germany. Crowds have turned up for a trip from West Stanley to South Shields but there are few children; perhaps they are on the buses. The heavy coats and hats of the crowds appear incongruous for August, so the people must have wrapped up well against a chill wind. If so, the travellers are in for a 'bracing' day on the beach.

By 1939, the QLs had been rebuilt with destination boxes in the roof. No 351 (centre) has a Q-type vertical windscreen, 389 a sloping one.
Beamish North of England Open Air Museum

build and 'up-and-at-'em' stance. Most QLs had a long afterlife. While a few went for further PSV service, many were sold off at £5 each to fields in the country and on the coast for use as summerhouses and holiday homes, often being driven there by Northern drivers. The author remembers whole fields of them near Crimdon on the Durham coast and the amazing site at Ellington in Northumberland which was only in the 1960s cleared of bus caravans. Indeed, Northern's first QL, 338, was rescued from such a site and is currently being restored at Beamish.

The year 1929 brought the 34-seat Madam or M-type SOS, still without luggage racks but offering more generously spaced and comfortable 'bucket' seats, the aim being to encourage women shoppers to travel to the bigger towns with a greater choice of retailers. Ransomes built the bodies on all 40 (428-67), the only modification being to fit roller-blind indicators in the roof.

For 1930, NGT had ordered 28 SOS COD buses and 12 XL coaches. BMMO, however, was going through a period of uncertainty, and its own XL coaches turned out to be over-bodied and unsatisfactory. The buses were cancelled, but 10 SRR (**S**hort Bros **R**olls-**R**oyce) coaches were delivered in a red and maroon or black livery (472-81). These were the first all-enclosed and the first half-cab coaches, and they also introduced the SOS 'RR' 6.4-litre six-cylinder engine and a new flat-top radiator.

The four-cylinder SOS was on its last legs in 1931, and still on a straight-frame chassis, when 10 IM (Improved Madam) buses (536-45 with Short Bros bodies) joined the 1930 prototype (471). This was a slightly bigger M with new radiator, but the weight increased to nearly 5 tons. They lasted until the late-1940s, and 540 still survives today.

BMMO had introduced the six-cylinder RR engine into buses as well as coaches, and for 1931 Northern bought 10 IM6 buses (546-55). The IM6s were fitted with route boards for the Newcastle–Liverpool express, so it was no surprise, perhaps, that the 1932 order for 10 IM6s described them as 'special long-distance IM omnibuses'. At £1,250 each, these represented a big saving when compared with the

SRR coaches at £1,786. Tynemouth/Wakefield's bought two IM6 in 1933, and Sunderland District had four in 1931 (100-3).

In 1932 came the greatest oddity of all; BMMO hired to Northern a new REDD — or strictly DD(RE) — rear-entrance double-deck bus with 52-seat Short Bros body, with an option to purchase at £1,780. NGT did so, and HA 8002 entered the fleet as No 593 in September 1933. The six-cylinder petrol engine was replaced by a BMMO oil engine in 1945, after which the chassis received a new Northern Coachbuilders body.

The final flowering of the SOS fleet came in 1934, with Northern's authorisation for the purchase of 14 six-cylinder 27ft 6in-long single-deckers from BMMO. The length is significant, as the permitted length of two-axle buses had just been increased. In December the order was clarified as 12 34-seat and two 38-seat buses at £1,430 each, all being the ON (**on**ward) model. The two 38-seaters went to Wakefield's Motors (W68/9) and the Northern batch were Nos 609-20. Sunderland District also bought 10 (124-33) which ran latterly as 38-seaters, the BMMO engine being

very compact. So ended the purchase of new BMMO chassis, on the best possible note. Two questions remain, however. What does SOS stand for, and why did purchase stop in 1934? Neither can be fully answered, but there are some clues.

Wyndham Shire was often asked what SOS meant, and his answer was always opaque. 'Shire's Omnibus Specification' is a reasonable guess. Gordon Hayter was to pay full tribute — 'the most practical of all omnibus designers, Mr Wyndham Shire, designed his famous SOS bus for the Midland Red company… It was certainly a remarkable vehicle, weighing only 3 tons 15cwt, it carried 32 passengers in comfort and gave a fuel consumption of 8 to 10mpg.' The 10 years of SOS buses had produced such a stable of 336 excellent vehicles that it must have taken a marked policy shift to move from them. No reason has ever been given for this in view of the high regard in which the SOS chassis was held at Northern. The possibility is that Gordon Hayter was turning to design himself and doing a 'Wyndham Shire' at Northern. The SOS story was by no means over!

3. Expansion and Competition, 1926-9

Worswick Street bus station, Newcastle, c1935. Buses entered at the bottom left and not downwards into the bays from Worswick Street as intended because Newcastle Corporation refused to allow buses to turn right on the Great North Road from Pilgrim Street into Worswick Street. The first bus is 604, the first production SE6 bus, which would be converted to two-axle in 1941 (and still survives today after a spell in the British Transport Commission Museum at Clapham from 1955). Beyond that are an SDO 1929 Leyland Tiger and Northern SOS M and ON buses. At the time of writing, the building still stands near the centre of Newcastle but has not been used, other than for Metro Taxis, for some years.
Go North East

In January 1926 a new Assistant General Manager from BMMO, John Petrie, was appointed. R. W. Cramp, the existing General Manager, then approaching retirement age, resigned and moved to take over the running of the Tynemouth company, and Petrie took over fully at Bensham in March.

Negotiations with rival operators fully engaged the Manager and directors. The first of these was with the Sunderland District Transport Co (successor to the Electric Tramways) in June 1925 over competition in the Hetton-le-Hole area and in particular the duplication of departure times from termini. The managing directors of the two companies agreed to let their respective managers work out an agreement, but SDT then offered to sell the company rather than implement such an agreement. An offer to purchase on the basis of an accord between the companies was made to the Receiver of the SDT company (*Commercial Motor* reporting in 1926 said the deal was done), but the debenture-holders eventually decided not to accept (presumably on the basis that the SDT company was at a low ebb but that a profitable and valuable operation could be built up) but to place the assets into a new company, the Sunderland District Omnibus Co Ltd, formed in 1927. Negotiations were broken off and competition resumed, particularly over the Houghton-le-Spring–Chester-le-Street and Houghton–Sunderland direct (via the A690, not the circuitous tramway route) services over which Northern already ran! With the SDO and its energetic new General Manager, Ernest Mountain, investing heavily in new Leyland PLSC Lion buses and selling off its old solid-tyred Bristols, battle was joined. It was now blue SDO Lion against red Northern SOS Q and QL.

A depot in the southeast of the operating area had become necessary with increased competition. Hetton-le-Hole was considered as a base, but land was eventually bought at Murton and a 45-bus garage opened in August 1926. Also in the east, Sunderland Corporation agreed to the use of a bus stand in Park Lane as the terminus of the Murton service. This large open space was relatively near the shops and town centre (and tram services to the beaches), had easy access to the southbound roads out of Sunderland and proved a good area for open bus stands, being adopted as the main 'company' terminus.

With the success of the purpose-built Gateshead bus station, NGT turned its thoughts to the provision of dedicated bus stations for the main termini, particularly with major new road plans in the late 1920s.

Durham was a congested small town with narrow main roads passing through the Market Place, which the developing bus services of the 1920s could swamp as a terminus. Northern planned a bus station in Durham early in 1926 and reached agreement to park buses on the part-demolished Hills Mill in North Road. In June 1927 the site was bought, plans were prepared and Groves of Chester-le-Street was engaged to construct the new station, which required considerable earthworks to provide turning and parking space. The station, with its cast-iron-and-glass canopies, opened in March 1929.

Newcastle was next to receive attention. Major new roads were planned, with a new bridge to carry the Great North Road across the Tyne to supplement the congested High Level Bridge, together with a new arterial route from Newcastle to the coast near Tynemouth and Whitley Bay, by-passing the congestion on roads along the north bank of the Tyne.

Firstly, however, Northern sought a physical base in Newcastle for its growing touring and excursion work. A garage, offices and booking hall (for excursion traffic only) were erected in 1927 on the Cross House site on Westgate Road. With the opening of Worswick Street bus station in 1929 and offices and booking points in nearby Pilgrim Street, the need for the Westgate Road premises declined; the site was leased back to Newcastle Corporation in September 1933 and a cinema erected.

Meanwhile a planned new bridge over the Tyne would open a much clearer and faster way into the centre of Newcastle, and land was sought on the southern edge of the commercial centre to give good access to the south and southeast. By May 1928, land at Worswick Street and Carliol Square was accepted by Newcastle's planning authority for use as a bus station, although services across the new Tyne Bridge were not sanctioned. The Watch Committee clearly had another priority — to develop the Corporation's own bus station in the Marlborough Crescent / Sheepmarket area (to the west of the Central railway station). This was quite close to the toll-bound Redheugh Bridge for services to Stanley and Consett and had good access along Scotswood Road for westerly traffic. There was one drawback: the approach from the Redheugh was under a low railway bridge — no double-deckers!

With the new Tyne Bridge due to open on 10 October 1928, Northern was becoming fretful in September. Neither the Gateshead nor Newcastle authorities had granted licences to operate bus services over the new bridge! Clearly this was only a matter of time, so the Worswick Street site was developed and, from the day of opening, six services were extended from Gateshead to the Worswick/Carliol site. But why Gateshead, when services from the south had been operating over the congested and narrow High Level Bridge? Northern and Newcastle Corporation had been at odds over the increasing bus traffic. In June 1926 Northern had appealed to the Ministry of Transport over the Corporation's refusal to issue licences for services. Congestion must have been

serious, as, in September, Northern, at the request of Newcastle, discontinued bus services over the bridge and, presumably, terminated at the new Gateshead bus station, with passengers continuing to Newcastle by tramcar.

By April 1929, however, Northern and Tynemouth had gained almost 200 licences to operate over the new Tyne Bridge and were discussing with the Corporation the use of Marlborough Crescent on the basis of 1 shilling per bus per day. Relations with Sunderland District had warmed again, and the chairmen of both companies had met and instructed their managers to make working arrangements, reduce competition and accept each other's return tickets. In June SDO (and Castle Motor Services) would

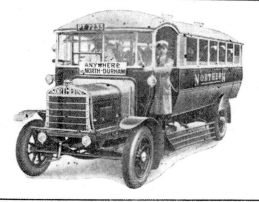

NORTHERN

OMNIBUS SERVICE GUIDE

To all parts of North Durham.

WHERE TO GO

AND

HOW TO GET THERE.

Frequent Reliable Services Daily.

See Map inside for connections together with first
and Last Buses with maximum interval of Service.

THE NORTHERN GENERAL TRANSPORT CO. LTD.,

Local Head Office :-Picktree Lane, Chester-le-St., Co. Durham, 'phone 125 &126.

BRANCH GARAGES—BENSHAM, Queen Street	Phone 1091 Gateshead
,, ,, CONSETT, Leadgate Road	,, 110 Consett
,, ,, MURTON, North View	,, 12 Murton
,, ,, STANLEY, West Stanley	,, 38 Stanley
,, ,, SUNDERLAND, Holmside	,, 700 Sunderland
OMNIBUS STATIONS—GATESHEAD, Wellington Street	,, 487 Gateshead
,, ,, DURHAM, North Road	
WAITING ROOMS —LOW FELL, Tram Terminus	
,, ,, HEWORTH, Tram Terminus	,, 92 Heworth

Printed by T. D. Stoddart, The City Printing Works, Chester-le-Street.

be allowed to use the Worswick station, when completed, at the 'Marlborough' price.

Worswick Street bus station opened in 1929 and immediately ran into a serious problem compounded by the steep gradient of the street and the falling land to the Carliol Square parking area at the bottom of the hill. The bus stands were arranged in an echelon diagonal to an exit road at the back of the long and narrow station. The intention was that buses would enter Newcastle over the new Tyne Bridge, turning right in Pilgrim Street and using the bus station bays downhill. Newcastle Corporation would not hear of this and forbade the right turn off the A1. Buses had thus to turn right at the end of the Tyne Bridge into City Road, then left under the Manors Arches (carrying the main Newcastle–Edinburgh railway line) and up and over into Carliol Square, entering uphill into the echelon stands. Exit was directly into Worswick Street and Pilgrim Street, and this had the merit of reducing traffic in both. There was, however, a major drawback. The road under the Arches was wide, and, as the road rose to Manors station, drivers swung left off City Road with as much speed as they could muster. The arches were high enough for a double-decker in the centre but not near the pavement. Newcastle, Northern's major centre, was now out-of-bounds to double-deckers from the southeast and southwest (not that the company possessed any in 1929). Also, because of the steepness of the stands, scotches had to be used for stationary buses when unloading and loading. The sights and sounds of conductors removing chocks and swinging onto a groaning, fully-laden postwar Guy Arab or AEC Regent double-decker as it juddered out of the stand between lines of waiting passengers made it one of the great bus station spectacles of Britain for the transport enthusiast, even if less so for the driver — not to mention the waiting passengers queuing across Worswick Street, with buses at full throttle passing within inches! The Worswick name, incidentally, was derived from that of a priest at St Andrew's Church, opposite the bus station.

The building programme of 1928/9 continued with a major new depot at South Shields. This was in use by the end of October 1929, with a formal opening on 21 November.

Services

The period up to the end of 1929 saw a great increase of infilling and linking services to accompany the large intake of SOS buses. In the Consett area there were new routes to Newcastle, via Dipton in 1926 and via Blackhill in 1929. Gateshead was still the major terminus for new services to Monkwearmouth (1926) and South Shields via Jarrow (1927) and via White Mare Pool (1928). Durham–Sunderland and Sunderland–South Shields were linked in 1928, albeit temporarily, and Sunderland–West Hartlepool was instituted the same year after Northern pressure on United. Signposts for the future were the short-lived (1928/9) limited-stop services from Newcastle to Bishop Auckland via Durham and to Stockton and Middlesbrough. In 1928 Sunderland Corporation asked Northern to run three services until it purchased buses to supplement the trams; one of these — the Castletown service beyond the Borough boundary — survived. Major developments were the start of a Newcastle–Leeds–Manchester–Liverpool 'daily tour' in May 1928 (following Northern's October 1927 application to Newcastle for licences to operate to Glasgow and Edinburgh also) and, with the opening of the new coast road, a joint Tynemouth / Wakefield's / Newcastle Corporation service to North Shields, introduced on 1 July 1929 from Newcastle's Haymarket bus station. In October 1927 Tynemouth had started services from Newcastle to Whitley Bay (joint with United) and from Newcastle to Tynemouth (with Wakefield's Motors).

In comparison with United, which surrounded Northern's operating area, NGT appears to have been more effective in squeezing out competitive small operators. Only two were bought out — Hallett's of Pelton, operating three buses between Murton and Durham in 1928, and Hunter's of Hebburn, running three between Newcastle and Jarrow, in 1929.

Relations with United

E. B. Hutchinson had set up United Automobile Services Ltd in 1912 in Lowestoft but, as a visionary, had foreseen potential demand in busy industrial areas and established operating bases up the East Coast, including Bishop Auckland in 1912 and Blyth, Northumberland, in 1919. After World War 1 it expanded rapidly and aggressively, taking over many small competitors. To reduce competition, Northern and United entered into territorial and through-running agreements.

The agreement of 1928/9 centred on Durham and on Newcastle. In County Durham, the dividing line ran roughly east–west from Easington on the coast, through Durham to near Tow Law in the west. In Northumberland, Tynemouth & District's area was southeast of a line drawn from Newcastle to Whitley Bay. Such agreements endured formally or informally until the sale of the BET group in 1968 and the formation of the National Bus Company. While co-operation persisted, there is no doubt that at times, Northern and Tynemouth had difficulty with United's conduct, which persisted long after the sale of United to the London & North Eastern Railway and Tilling & British Automobile Traction Ltd in August 1929 (and there were BET-appointed Directors on the Board of TBAT). A particular source of friction had been the competition encountered by Tynemouth Tramways between Blyth and Tynemouth in 1920, and this and other 'incursions' in Northumberland rumbled on without complete resolution until at least 1938. The agreement also suffered considerable strain from 1929 onwards with the purchase by both parties of operators straddling the 'Durham line'.

Northern was thus hemmed in by the leap-frogging United, but there was an area not covered by the agreement — roughly that to the west of the Tow Law–Consett–Newcastle-River Tyne arc. North and south of the Tyne Valley was rural land, probably of little interest to Northern, which had built up rural services southwest of Consett and Lanchester, but the Tyne Valley itself presented an expansion opportunity, and Northern's Keswick service ran along this corridor. Newcastle Corporation's blue buses ran south of the river to Hexham, but Robert Emmerson's services to Hexham and Carlisle were open to offer. Northern opened negotiations and agreed in October 1928 to form a new private company with Emmerson, part-financed by shares in the new company. This was not to be, however. Emmerson broke off negotiations in November and entered talks with the LNER, which from August 1928 was allowed to take a financial interest in bus operators. The LNER was successful, but NGT did not give up. In October 1929 it tried to buy the LNER shareholding in Emmerson's but was again thwarted, as the LNER decided to pass the Emmerson business to United (in January 1930), which would later take over the remains of Newcastle Corporation's Tyne Valley services. The door was shut, the 'opposition' had won, and Northern had to concentrate on its defined and limited but lucrative territory.

4. Consolidation, 1929-39

▶ In the late 1920s the 'Big Four' railway companies created by the 1923 Grouping were increasingly threatened by competition from buses and long-distance coaches, and in August 1928 they were given powers to purchase competitors. The LNER was facing severe independent competition on the remains of the pioneer North Eastern Railway bus services from Durham. The NER had started running buses in 1903 but in the NGT area from South Shields southwards in 1907 with double-deckers and in 1908 from Blyth to Whitley Bay. These services ceased during the war, but Durham, from 1912, proved to be a more reliable base. The Durham services were the most intensive routes inherited from the NER and included those to Sacriston and Lanchester, Blackhill and Shotley Bridge in Northern territory from a garage near the southbound platform at Durham railway station.

In September 1928 Northern was forced to reduce fares to match 'drastic' fare reductions on some railway bus services, and, with developments clearly expected, NGT and LNER met to discuss services. A year later, LNER's intention to buy shares in NGT and to come to service agreements were clear. Wakefield's Motors Ltd of North Shields passed to Northern in 1929 (with Northern acquiring six AEC buses and two Daimlers), with the LNER taking an equal shareholding to BET in the NGT Group, and the Durham operations would pass to NGT and United in January 1930 (with Northern buying six apple-green-and-white Thornycroft buses). The NGT fleet was then fitted with LNER information boxes, and timetables gave details of train services. There was also inter-availability of return tickets.

Wakefield's Motors Ltd had been set up by Thomas Wakefield in September 1927 with subscribers T. W. and H. Brook of Stockton and J. Hodge of Galashiels (also Directors of Eastern Express) to run bus services. Wakefield was a motor engineer, agent (for Thornycroft and Dennis) and hirer of taxis and charabancs in North Shields, and his hire business was sold to the Company in 1928.

Wakefield's Motors was placed under Tynemouth control, and all coaching/excursion traffic was handled under the Wakefield's name. Some bus service licences continued to be held by Wakefield's, so the 'WAKEFIELDS' fleetname appeared on double-deckers, as well as all coaches, until the 1960s.

The 1930 Road Traffic Act transferred the licensing of services to a national framework of regional Traffic Commissioners. This effectively enhanced the value of established services. Early in 1930, the General County Omnibus Co Ltd, of Birtley, reached an agreement for the sale of its services and 36 buses to Northern. General County had started as a consortium of 20 or so individual operators in the Chester-le-Street and Birtley areas, organised by J. A. Kay, who had registered the company in 1927. They competed with NGT on the Newcastle–Durham 'main line' but, as they were not bound by the UAS/NGT agreement, had extended services to Stockton and Middlesbrough, to Bishop Auckland and to Esh Winning and Waterhouses. In March 1930 the buy-out was complete, and NGT set up its own GCOC Ltd to which the vehicles were sold. GCOC Ltd continued as an associated company until 1936, when it was wound up. The services became the 54 (Newcastle–Esh Winning) and the well-known 55 (Newcastle–Middlesbrough) and 56 (Newcastle–Bishop Auckland).

In February 1930 the new GCOC attempted to reach agreement with United over the operations south of Durham, with United to

be paid receipts less expenses. After many months United rejected this and took a shareholding and some of the buses. However, the 55 and 56 were to be jointly worked by United and GCOC until 1936, when NGT took over the GCOC workings.

Also in February, Northern bought Castle Motor Services (Stobie & Currie) with seven buses and a Newcastle–South Shields service that became part of the famous 6. In June ABC (Atkinson & Browell of Consett), which operated from Consett to Newcastle via Blackhill with 10 buses (mainly Leyland Lion PLSCs), sold out to NGT.

Meanwhile Northern was complaining repeatedly to United about the latter's purchase of Eastern Express Motors Ltd of West Hartlepool, which ran services to Newcastle through NGT territory and even had a depot there at Hetton-le-Hole. Northern requested that United withdraw these services in January 1930 when United took over. Eventually NGT part-purchased Eastern with United and took over 23 buses and the Hetton premises, a former theatre, which it then let. The Eastern fleet was quite new, with Associated Daimlers and AECs.

Further friction arose from United's service to Keswick, which competed with Northern's. United withdrew on condition that Northern would not carry short-distance passengers up to Hexham. There was further discussion about United's Newcastle–High Spen service (allowed) and its extension of its London–Middlesbrough service to Sunderland and then Newcastle (United not to carry local passengers). A happier settlement was that of the inter-availability of return tickets on the two Newcastle–West Hartlepool services (operated by United and Sunderland District).

The year 1931 brought the biggest expansion of all. The directors of the Sunderland District Omnibus Co Ltd accepted the sale of the shares to Northern, but the business was retained as a separate entity, with independent management (Ernest Mountain), livery and strong local identity for this 100-strong fleet (based at Philadelphia), whose vehicle maintenance and presentation were of the highest quality. Considerable independence was allowed in vehicle design and purchase, and the fleet provided a fascinating comparison with Northern's.

Soon after this, General County bought G. W. Hetherington & Co Ltd of Coundon — which (as A1) ran from Bishop Auckland to Newcastle and to Sunderland — on behalf of Northern, SDO and United. The services were apportioned between the three operators.

After negotiation with Tynemouth Council, the unprofitable Tynemouth tramway finally closed after partial substitution by single-deck buses in August 1931. A new fleet of smart AEC Regent double-deckers (some Wakefield's) was introduced. The Blyth service continued as a joint service with United. Because of the financial state of Tynemouth & District, Northern had to assist in the purchase of new buses for T&D.

Northern's foothold in Sunderland was confirmed in 1932 with the joint operation with Sunderland Corporation of the service to Castletown.

There was a spate of acquisitions in 1934, starting with the joint purchase (with United) of Ennis & Reed Ltd of Crook and its Newcastle service. This sealed the running of the through joint services south of Durham with United under a new 1934 agreement.

In the same year, the substantial firm of Prinn of Sunniside, running buses from West Stanley to Newcastle, sold its business. The consortium trading as White & Nixon of Chester-le-Street contributed 15 buses and that idiosyncratic service running diagonally across Northern's territory, the 62 from Esh Winning to South Shields. The 1930s, however, had not been good years for the core business. With the slump following the financial crash in the USA in 1929, the heavy industries of shipbuilding, iron and steel and coal suffered massive losses of business, with consequent unemployment and reduced travel.

Another subsidiary came into the fold in January 1936 with the purchase, with SDO, of the shareholding of the Tyneside Tramways & Tramroads Co of Wallsend, which ran the 18 or so buses which had replaced the trams in 1930. Starting off with reconditioned ex-Southdown Tilling-Stevens double-deckers, it had standardised on Leyland Titans, including three owned by Newcastle Corporation (following its share of joint Newcastle/Tyneside tram service). Tyneside, with its green livery and services from North Shields to Newcastle (Croft Street) via Riverside, and Gosforth, was maintained by Northern as a separate entity. As with SDO, the independent purchasing of Leylands continued.

The same year John Petrie retired. Gordon Hayter took over as General Manager as well as Chief Engineer and was assisted by the strong team of James Forster as Traffic Manager and Donald Sinclair as Assistant Engineer.

Charlton's Blue Safety Coaches Ltd of Hebburn was next to sell its bus business to Northern, in 1936, United already having purchased the long-distance coach services earlier. A total of 21 buses and services in the South Shields area were involved.

In 1935 Northern had been interested in Robson Bros of Consett, but the successful buyer had been Venture (Reed Bros). The latter, however, indicated its willingness to sell out in 1937, but Northern and United (whose Northumberland operations were now adjacent) would not meet the price. The business reformed as Venture Transport (Newcastle) Ltd in 1938 and continued as a large and well-respected independent operator until 1970.

The final prewar purchase, of T. Cook of Consett in 1939, was complicated by United's inability to obtain licences for its part of the proposed joint buy-out of the Consett–Tow Law and Consett–Stanhope rural services. Northern, on its own, went ahead with buying the sections of service to Tow Law.

In vehicle terms the 1930s was to prove the most spectacular decade in the Company's history and saw the best of the late-1920s buses (Leyland Lion and SOS QL) transformed into comfortable, reliable and economical buses and elegant coaches which have rarely been matched.

Northern had been wedded to Daimler and then SOS products since inception, with the addition of some AEC/ADC buses. Leylands had been tried (and swiftly sold, probably in the interests of standardisation), but other suppliers to BET, such as Dennis and Tilling-Stevens, had not. However, Gordon Hayter reported in 1930 that '43 buses' were unsatisfactory when taken into stock. These included the ADC 416, AEC 426 and AEC Reliance (many ex-Eastern and Wakefield's and only two or three years old). Engines were unreliable because of unsatisfactory workmanship at the factory. Front hubs failed repeatedly, and cone clutches led to poor driver control and transmission wear and vibration. SOS hubs and clutches were fitted and the Dodson, Hall Lewis and Strachan bodies required reconstruction. These

buses kept the Bensham works busy overhauling them in 1930 and 'reconstructing' them in 1931. The NGT Board was unhappy at the high cost of reconstruction, at £400 per bus, but the 'Northernised' Reliances eventually had long lives.

In 1931/2 Gordon Hayter modernised a batch of Leyland Lion PLSCs taken over from ABC into what was effectively Northern's 'standard' bus, with extended chassis, short cab, Lockheed brakes and a new 38-seat light Short Bros body. NGT did not buy new PLSCs but would have been well acquainted with that excellent chassis and considered the investment of £700 per bus worthwhile.

The side-engined chassis

Gordon Hayter, however, wanted more from his buses — more seats, better components and easier maintenance. If the market would not provide them, he would build them himself. Bensham now moved up a gear. In October 1932 the NGT Board authorised the construction of a 'special six-wheel chassis to carry a 46-seat body, at £750'. The body, at £525, was authorised in April 1933. The innovative design was to the maximum dimensions of the period and hence used three axles and placed a Hercules side-valve petrol engine behind the front axle; as the engine was compact in height and substantially under the floor, this freed up the floor space for seating. Northern No 586 (chassis No NGT64), with a lightweight Short Bros body seating 45, was the SE6 (**S**ide **E**ngine **6** wheels) prototype and went to work successfully on the Newcastle–South Shields service 6.

Five more SE6s were sanctioned in November 1933, at £1,535 each — a modest cost compared with the 1934 SOS ONs at £1,430 and the 1935 AEC Regals at £1,471. However, AEC objected that the SE infringed its Q-type patents, which were

Chester-le-Street depot always had a large fleet of NGT SE6 buses and coaches to look after, as well as the coaches. All the buses had been converted from Hercules WXC-2 petrol engines to AEC 6.6-litre ex-tank oil engines after the war — more noise, less speed. All side pillars were raked, and in 1934 they were among the first buses in the country to employ this feature. In March 1951 Short Bros-bodied 672, one of the 1935 batch assembled by AEC, still retains its original radiator grille (yes, the radiator was behind it!) and large fleetname. Drivers gained access via the heavy offside door hinged from the front pillar. The scene is North Burns, Chester-le-Street, with the stand for the Coventry express in the background. 'Trading Estate' refers to Team Valley in Gateshead, indicating a short, workman's journey. *A. Cross*

Having withdrawn its 1919-21 Daimler double-deckers, the Group took to the new double-decker with little enthusiasm, despite the success of the lowbridge Leyland Titan elsewhere. Major Hayter never really accepted the value of the concept other than for city work but needed the extra capacity for intensive workings, given the restricted length of single-deckers. The new double-deck operations in 1930 with demonstrators centred on Sunderland and, particularly, from 1931, Tynemouth, where the new AEC Regents such as T39 replaced the trams between North Shields and Whitley Bay. The new petrol-engined Regents were handsome 50-seaters with Short Bros bodies and would have long lives. 'Tram Service' legends were applied to them when new, but what was their livery? Up to 1928, at least, Northern buses were red and white; by 1934 they were red and cream. Was cream was introduced on these 1931/2 Northern and Tynemouth double-deckers?
Ian Allan Library

Brush-bodied AEC Regent CN 5242 of 1932 exemplified the fascination of the Group fleets. New to Northern as 564, it was quickly transferred to Tynemouth as T50 and repainted in the 'cream window' livery. In 1941 it was transferred to Tyneside Tramways as TT27 and its only AEC. Converted to oil engine, it was rebodied in 1946 with a new 56-seat body by Northern Coachbuilders, and was transferred back to Northern in 1951 as No 1403, being finally sold in 1956. A life of 24 years shows the quality of the Regent chassis. This rear view, with prominent 'Shop at Binns' advertisement — effectively part of the livery — reveals the inset short platform on these buses. The white oval enamel plate is the hackney plate, carried by all PSVs from 1931 to 1939, and bears the Crown, the Ministry of Transport number for the bus and the letter 'A' for the Northern Traffic Area. Preservationists will note the magnificent rear lighting display of one red bull's-eye lamp. *Go North East*

widely drawn to include two- and three-axle chassis with a variety of drive-train arrangements. Northern made an offer to take a licence to build from AEC with a royalty of 1 guinea per bus and to plate the chassis accordingly. Northern's design team of Donald Sinclair and W. G. Allen, however, had one more ace to play. The 1934 batch saw the front axle set back to allow a front entrance and the first modern single-decker was born — 44 seats, all facing forward, engine under the floor (at the side) and driver overview of the entrance. The door was placed at the side of the driver, sliding across the front of the saloon. Short Bros built the sleek, sloping-pillar bodywork without luggage racks. The driver reached his seat via an offside door. While the AEC Q double-decker introduced the front entrance, the front-entrance Q single-decker did not arrive until 1936, and, with the tall AEC engine, the interior of the Q was always untidy unless a high floor (for coaching only) were adopted. Northern solved the wheel-arch problem by using a sunken gangway, with seats on a ramped floor. It is also arguable that the SE was better 'engineered for purpose' than the Q. With a radiator at the front of the bus, overheating problems which plagued the Q were avoided, and the engine air intake was quickly moved from the engine bay to take clean air from the roof. The SE6s were converted to oil engines with AEC 6.6-litre A172 and ex-Army A183 engines without disrupting the seating. SE6 weak points were the single-drive rear bogie, which could give poor adhesion on greasy cobbles, and the low position of the gearbox, which could be damaged on uneven ground.

No fewer than 31 SE6s were sanctioned for 1935, and AEC agreed to build up the chassis, which would have swamped Bensham. Of these, 25 were bodied as 44-seat buses (five being for Tynemouth) and six were magnificent 28-seat coaches by Short Bros which carried a premium of £110 per body. For 1936 there were two more coaches (by Beadle) and three buses for Tynemouth which ended SE6 production at 42 chassis.

Return of the double-decker

Commercial Motor magazine had reported in 1922 that the Consett–Stanley and Stanley–Newcastle services were operated by double-deckers, and passengers were said to have to 'lower their heads at Eden Pit and King's Bridge, Annfield Plain'. Inevitably someone didn't, and off came the 'deckers.

The advent of the Leyland Titan, which revolutionised inter-urban traffic elsewhere, passed Northern by initially, but, with Tynemouth tramway losing money, two double-deckers were obtained in 1930 for evaluation. Both were registered locally — BR 8379 (all-Leyland Titan TD1) and CN 4520 (AEC Regent with Short Bros body). The 'highbridge' AEC Regent was chosen, and Northern/Tynemouth placed orders. In 1931/2 the Tynemouth trams were replaced by 16 Regents with Short Bros bodywork, of which four were for Wakefield's, and these handsome machines offered quiet, speedy and comfortable travel as some of the best vehicles of their day. Northern ordered eight

SHORT BROS : (ROCHESTER & BEDFORD) LTD.

OF
**ROCHESTER
KENT**

BUILDERS OF RELIABLE BODIES.

FOR
PASSENGER COMFORT   DRAUGHTLESS VENTILATION
BRILLIANT LIGHTING AND SUPERLATIVE FINISH
SPECIFY
SHORT BROS : BODY WORK

Telephone : Chatham 2861.   Telegrams : "Seaplanes" Rochester.

Regents with Brush bodies (562-9), of which 569 was on the longer, 26ft chassis and had a very modern 60-seat body. After evaluating a Titan TD1, SDO ordered 10 Brush-bodied Regents.

So where did these double-deckers work, if they couldn't get into the Newcastle bus stations? Sunderland, which was relatively free of low bridges, had to be the base, and the first Northern 'deckers ran from Murton depot on the Sunderland–Dawdon/Easington Lane 21 and 23 services. SDO ran from Sunderland to New Silksworth and to Easington Lane via Houghton. The Sunderland–South Shields 14 service was converted to double-deck operation in 1933 with forward-entrance Regents — three with Short Bros 'draughtless' lowbridge (why?) bodies for South Shields depot and three with unsatisfactory Brush highbridge bodies for SDO. Tynemouth was to get three forward-entrance but highbridge Short Bros draughtless Regents in 1935.

In 1931 Northern had hired (and later bought) a demonstration oil-engined Regent, MY 2102, which was also sent to Murton. This was an historic bus, built with a petrol engine but converted to oil with AEC's first production oil engine, A155/1. The Short Bros body was a 50-seater and may have been open-staircase, although it is difficult to believe that, if so, Northern would have run it until wartime without enclosing the staircase. The BMMO REDD double-decker (593) also joined the Murton fleet after hire.

The 1938 order for Tyneside of nine TD5s was a large one (for Tyneside), and, if the chassis was to then-current NGT Group policy, the choice of coachbuilder was a surprise — the Group had not previously patronised Eastern Coach Works at all. The Charles Roe-derived ECW bodies were, however, to a high standard, and the batch survived intact for 16 years. The livery of sage green and cream was lined out in gold and black; the 'TYNESIDE' script was white. No 22, like many of the batch, ended up with a showman.
R. Marshall collection

The 10 Weymann-bodied AEC Regents of 1940, shared between Northern and Tynemouth, were smart machines which set the pattern for Tynemouth's postwar fleet. The 91 service was introduced between Consett and Durham in 1949, replacing the 'Witbank' operation based at Lanchester. Worked from Consett depot, it was the most rural of Northern's 'decker services, being operated usually by elderly AEC Regents until the mid-'Fifties, when Guy Arabs took over and some of the charm departed. No 961 leaves Lanchester for Durham in 1949.
G. Turner / Photobus

Reservations, shared with United, about the inter-urban operation of double-deckers must have re-surfaced in 1934, when Gordon Hayter wrote of his dissatisfaction with the double-decker other than for short-distance town transport unless it could seat 60 (which 569 could). Northern offered 20 AEC Regents with Brush and Short bodies for sale in *Commercial Motor* in November 1934, but none departed.

The next 'decker was a surprise: the first new Leyland for 15 years and an ex-demonstration Titan TD3c with Weymann forward-entrance body, TJ 4511 (No 699). Perhaps Gordon Hayter, with his interest in transmission systems, wanted to try a torque-converter Leyland! It was quickly sent to join TD4c Titans at Tyneside in 1936 when Northern bought that company. In 1938 NGT and Hayter patented a centrifugal clutch which was built by AEC and at least 24 used on London Transport buses experimentally.

Further forward-entrance double-deckers were three (AEC) in 1937 and, in 1938, eight (Leyland) for Tynemouth and five (Leyland) for Northern. Two ex-Ribble Titan TD1s were bought and reconditioned for Murton in 1939. There was a big intake in 1939/40 with war looming, all rear-entrance — 11 Weymann-bodied Regents for Northern/Tynemouth, nine Titan TD5s with ECW bodies for Tyneside and five TD7s with Roe bodies for SDO. By 1940 the group ran 109 double-deckers, with Tyneside (26) entirely and Tynemouth/Wakefield's (37) primarily double-deck. SDO had 18 but Northern (28) had the lowest proportion, restricted to Sunderland/South Shields operations. This was to change.

Oil and gas power

Northern was quite late in exploring the apparent, then real benefits of oil engines in the early 1930s, perhaps because the use of double-deckers was itself a novelty in 1931. The first experimental diesel bus was MY 2102 on demonstration in 1931, which must have been successful.

In 1932 there were further experiments featuring Gardner and Dorman oil engines in SOS M chassis and AEC oil engines in AEC Reliances. AEC came out of this well, and the first new oil-engined chassis were six Regals in 1934 for Consett depot, with A165 8.8-litre units and Short bodies. Five Regals in 1935 for Stanley had A171 7.7-litre engines and Weymann bodies. The first new oil-engined double-deckers were Leyland TJ 4511 and Tynemouth T79-81 of 1935, and thereafter all double-deckers were diesels.

The early 1930s was a time of great hardship for the area. The production of coal, steel and ships all declined, and, with the exception of ICI at Billingham, there was little base for chemicals or the motor and aircraft industries which were developing elsewhere. Gordon Hayter, with his interest in innovation, tried experimentally to replace petrol with gas from coal, to assist local industry. In conjunction with the Northern Gas Board, coal-gas was compressed into cylinders mounted on an SOS QL chassis. Although

▲ In 1935 AEC introduced the medium-weight Regal II, with a new 6.6-litre oil engine. Northern bought 25 of the early production (chassis 0862003 upwards) and fitted them with BEF-style Weymann bodies — 36-seaters on the first 15 and more comfortable 34-seaters with half-length luggage racks on the final 10. The model drew complaints of failures and faults from almost all purchasers, which centred on the A172 oil engine. A 6.6-litre petrol version had to be rushed out to power the later chassis already constructed. Doubtless this was a considerable blow to AEC, which, judging by its attempts to sell 6.6-litre direct-injection underfloor-engined chassis for buses and for coaches to Northern in 1938, must have wished the 6.6-litre-engined Regal II and derivatives to be successors to the long-established Regal. Half of the batch were rebodied in 1946 by Pickering. No 716 is seen with its original Weymann body in March 1951 at Chester-le-Street *en route* for Sunderland. *A. Cross*

◄ In many ways the 1938/9 NGT SE4 40-seaters were the high-point of Northern production and a clear signpost for the PSV industry which would be taken up and developed by BMMO. These handsome and well-designed buses took over the flatter, intensive workings out of South Shields, in particular. English Electric built the Northern-designed bodies with all seats facing forward, and the door, which slid across the front bulkhead, can be clearly seen. Performance with the AEC 6.6-litre engine was adequate rather than sparkling. *Go North East*

achieving technical proficiency, the project was not developed, as the cost in electricity alone (to compress the gas) was greater than that of the equivalent petrol fuel.

AECs, SE4s and Leylands

With 34 or 36 seats in his new AEC Regals, Major Hayter considered in 1935 that the SE design could be developed as a two-axle maximum-capacity single-decker. The design allowed 40 seats, all facing forward, and in October 1935 the NGT Board gave authority to construct a prototype. No 701 was petrol-engined and worked sufficiently well for a production batch of 25 oil-engined buses to be authorised in January 1937 at £1,560 each (the oil-engined Regal batches had cost £1,470 and then £1,270 each). These handsome, well-designed buses were actually built in 1938/9, given Bensham's limited production space (and this, rather than cost, probably limited SE4 production). The oil engine selected was AEC's A172 6.6-litre, but this would have required considerable modification with accessible offside accessories for the side engine installation.

By now, the fleet was showing division between the upland areas of west Durham, which tended to be AEC garages, and the remainder, where lower-power buses congregated. All the SEs

were 'lowland' buses, and with the 6.6-litre diesel, not the swiftest of movers.

For 1936, AEC's new Regal II medium-weight chassis with the A172 engine was sampled. The model was unsuccessful, one of a series at AEC in the 1930s. Northern's 25 were sorted out, with the A172 being re-engineered and converted to direct-injection, but the model was dropped after complaints by customers. AEC tried to sell developments of the Regal II as an underfloor 6.6-litre direct-injection-engined bus or coach — virtually an AEC SE4 with radiator at the front. Northern 'adopted' the 6.6-litre engine, buying AEC jigs and spares (cheaply, no doubt) for this unloved engine, although the Army bought hundreds of twin sets of A183/4 engines for Matilda tanks.

Orders for 1937 reverted to the trusty Regal I (25 buses) but also included 10 Daimler COG5 pre-selector 34-seaters, which would have been a surprise had they been delivered. They weren't, and 10 more Regals with Wilson gearboxes took their place. The mechanical units from this batch were destined to have very long lives.

The potential threat to AEC in 1937 became real in 1938 with only two Regal coaches with magnificent Duple Coronation bodies on chassis with reconditioned petrol engines from Tynemouth Regents. The rest were Leylands — 32 TS8 buses and coaches and 13 TD5s, plus the Tyneside and SDO orders.

With the A173 7.7-litre available in the excellent Regal chassis, it was back to AEC in 1939 and 1940, and in a big way. As well as eight Regal coaches and one chassis (to replace a written-off 1937 Regal), there were no fewer than 92 Regal B 38-seater buses, including seven for Tynemouth. The Regal B was designed by NGT and AEC and combined the compact Regal II front end with a high ramped floor to limit wheel-arch intrusion to give 38 seats at £1,493. Scottish Motor Traction also bought the model. The buses, without luggage racks, were quite basic and were known as 'utilities' but, like the QL, were hard-worked go-anywhere buses. However, Robert Bailey, later Director and General Manager of Lancashire United, was not entirely convinced. The short engine bay meant the loss of the cooling fan, and the 'utilities' had a tendency to overheat. Northern now had an excellent fleet to face the war.

So what had Sunderland District been doing since 1931? After 'Northern-standard' AEC Regents and SOS IM and ON buses, Mr Mountain reverted to his own preference — Leyland. A pair of second-hand Tiger TS4s from Northern and then a superb fleet of 16 Tiger TS7s and 19 TS8s with Roe bodies formed the bus fleet. Meanwhile SDO bought its first-ever coach bodies and dressed them in pale blue and ivory — Duple rebodied 1929 TS1s 90-5 in 1937 and Burlingham two 1930 TS1s in 1939 (97/9), but all remained petrol-engined.

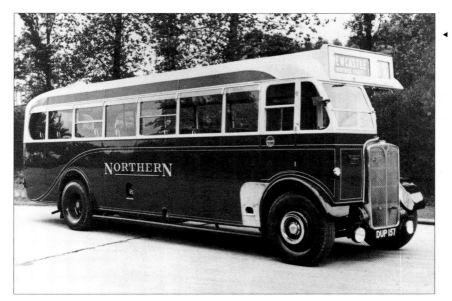

◄ AEC returned to favour for the large orders of 1939/40 with the Regal B chassis, its compact front end allowing a 38-seat body to be fitted. With the A173 7.7-litre engine now available and reliable, Northern's next 'go-anywhere' bus (after the SOS QL) was ready. The high, ramped-floor body design minimised wheel-arch intrusion, allowing forward-facing seats, and this design was used up to 1950. There were no luggage racks, and these fairly basic buses were known as 'Utilities' — a term later applied to wartime buses. One sacrifice was the engine fan. Northern and Tynemouth had 92 of these Regals, which, with the SOS, bore the brunt of wartime services. Bodies were by Brush, Weymann and, in the case of 907, English Electric.
R. Marshall collection

◄ Sunderland District built up an excellent fleet of 1930s Leyland Tigers, 16 TS7s and 19 TS8s, all with Roe bus bodies seating 32 or 35. No 136 is one of the 1936 batch with BEF-specification bodies. Delivered in very dark blue and white, it had its roof overpainted grey during the war. It is seen in Park Lane, Sunderland, in March 1951, waiting to depart to Ryhope over the old SDET tram route. Behind it is a 1940 Roe-bodied Leyland TD7, which will be working the short service to New Silksworth. Both buses were very much to Ernest Mountain's specification. No 136 would be withdrawn very soon once the Royal Tigers arrived.
A. Cross

6. Northern at War again

The threat of war with Germany, coupled with recovery from the 1930s Depression, led to increased activity in the munitions and military-hardware industries and their suppliers. The bitter early 'Thirties gave way to increasing financial security among skilled tradesmen, whose experience was needed, and car ownership became affordable for a growing minority. This was, however, against a background of apprehension over the seemingly inevitable conflict.

After September 1939, when war was declared, the whole population would be affected. The effects on the Group's operations were progressive. They included the prohibition of all long-distance and touring, to conserve fuel, tyres and labour; coaches were placed in store, some for the duration. Buses were requisitioned, some with their drivers, while others were converted for Civil Defence use as ambulances or, in the case of one AEC Reliance, a mobile operating theatre. Younger male staff were transferred to other essential work or called up. Conductors were trained as drivers, and many hundreds of female conductresses trained in their place. As petrol rationing was introduced and non-essential private motoring virtually ceased, passenger loadings increased, particularly for maximum effort in the shipyards, Royal Ordnance factories and new industrial trading estates.

The loss of requisitioned stock was met by bringing withdrawn buses out of store, ceasing to operate some services and withdrawing others earlier in the evening. Some buses, including SOS Ms, were converted to perimeter seating to increase standing capacity, and some coaches (such as the 'Liverpool' Brush-bodied 1938 Leyland TS8s) were converted to buses. Northern's build-up of double-deck capacity in 1939/40 served it well, but access to Worswick Street for double-deckers became essential.

In 1941 NGT persuaded Newcastle to build out the kerbs at the Manors arches, forcing buses to use the centre of the road; thus double-deckers could safely get into Worswick Street, and peak-time double-deck duplication of short workings (eg the 39 to Washington/Fatfield only) took some of the strain. The through services with United ceased at Durham and Easington Village, allowing each company to manage its affairs as best it

The Group was not a major user of the wartime bus, as its fleet was overwhelmingly single-deck and coped reasonably well. However, the wartime 'utility' double-deckers allocated, all Guy Arabs (six to SDO and 20 to Northern), did represent a considerable increase in the double-deck fleet. No 1063, a Northern Counties-bodied Arab of 1945, was one of the best wartime buses and is seen in March 1951, fully lined-out, unloading at Chester-le-Street on its way to Sacriston, near Durham. The Jeffrey's (of Edinburgh) beer advert was a rare one. In the background a 1946 AEC Regal with Saunders body waits to depart for Consett.
A. Cross

could and letting through passengers change buses for onward travel.

Many of the requisitioned buses were re-purchased in 1942/3 and with the relative dearth of double-deckers at Northern, 1932/3 AEC Regents from Tynemouth and Sunderland District were drafted across and a couple of Midland Red SOSs turned up with returning ex-War Department buses. A relatively small number of wartime 'utility' Guy Arab double-deckers were allocated — 20 to NGT and six to SDO. Tynemouth finally received five Northern Counties-bodied Guys in 1946 (T123-7) to a relaxed specification, and these ponderous but reliable buses were to have a big impact after the war. Meanwhile AEC was still the supplier of choice, and in 1943 NGT ordered 75 single-deckers and 50 double-deckers for delivery 'after hostilities ceased'.

◄ During the war, old AEC Regents from Tynemouth (six) and SDO (five) were sent to Northern, expanding the double-deck fleet still further. Nearly all were converted to oil engines and given wartime bodies built by Northern Coachbuilders at Cramlington airship shed in Northumberland. CN 5507, however, was one of Northern's own (No 574), originally fitted with a Short Bros lowbridge forward-entrance body. *Go North East*

Some of the bodies on the 1932/3 AEC Regents and Tyneside TD1s were getting into a parlous state, and the Ministry of Supply allocated new 'utility' bodies for construction at Northern Coachbuilders' Cramlington airship-shed. Regent 562 (CN 5240) received a new body built there entirely by female labour, and considerable publicity was given to this contribution to the War Effort. Many of the early petrol-engined Regents had been converted to oil with AEC 7.7-litre engines, and this programme was completed during the war.

While maintenance, particularly of bodies, had to be restricted, much of the fleet had to be painted into camouflage livery. Northern was unusual in adopting a dark, military green (in some cases with red fleetnames) rather than grey for repaints. Unrepainted buses were given grey roofs, but with some, particularly AEC Regals and SE buses, only the centre section of the roof was painted grey, leaving the domes in cream. As everywhere else, street lights

were out, vehicle lights were dimmed and sticky, blast-resistant netting was applied to windows, particularly the Guys. This made driving and conducting (particularly on the perimeter-seaters) difficult after dark, and more civilians were killed in road accidents than by enemy bombing. Even though strategic targets, such as the Tyneside shipyards and Sunderland, were heavily bombed, the Group fleets escaped lightly.

The SE6 buses had problems with spare parts for the rear bogies which had been manufactured locally. Northern applied to the Ministry of War Transport for permission to rebuild No 604 (the first front-entrance one) to two axles as a prelude to the conversion of the rest, but only the trial was allowed. When converted in 1941, 604, at 30ft long, did not meet contemporary Construction & Use Regulations, and its operation could be sanctioned only by the issue of a specific Statutory Instrument in 1942. The successful use of 604 was to lead directly to the 1950 relaxation of the length of two-axle single-deckers to 30ft.

Tynemouth continued its preference for AECs after the war. The Weymann-bodied Regent was the characteristic Tynemouth/Wakefield's double-decker. No T153 from the 1948 batch (143-56) is seen at Whitley Bay on the intensive ferry service. Behind is Wakefield's 1949 AEC Regent III 157 with NCB body; both are in fully lined-out livery with large fleetnames. Despite its many improvements, the Regent III was used only in single batches by Tynemouth and SDO. Perhaps Major Hayter thought them too powerful for their work. *D. F. Parker*

SDO kept faith with Roe-bodied Leylands after the war, with 1946 and 1947 batches of five Titan PD1s used to double-deck many services, including the 57 (Sunderland–Durham-Bishop Auckland), run jointly with United. No 184 is about to enter Park Lane bus station in October 1957 with a 49/95 working to Newcastle. This interworked with the through Newcastle–West Hartlepool service. By this time the SDO garter had been abandoned for a script fleetname as part of the Forster changes. The single-line destination had been extended to two lines of small script. *R. L. Kell*

34

7. After the War, 1946-54

Having served the region very effectively during the war, when both staff and vehicles were hard-pressed, Northern had to absorb returning staff, resume its long-distance services and excursions and reintroduce suspended operations. A strike in March 1945 over new schedules led to the temporary substitution of Army lorries in place of buses. The fleet had suffered, and with many of the faithful SOS fleet approaching 20 years of work, urgent upgrading was needed. The volume of work required on bus bodies exceeded the Company's capabilities, and, over the next five years, much was placed with outside coachbuilders.

Gordon Hayter initially retained AEC as major supplier but turned to Guy Motors to provide special chassis for the 38-seat body and standard chassis for double-deckers with a new body supplier, Northern Coachbuilders. Sunderland District and Tyneside continued their allegiance to Leyland, and even Tynemouth/Wakefield's maintained its independence with a fleet of 29 Weymann-bodied Regents in 1946 and 1948. The eight much-improved Regent IIIs with NCB bodies of 1949 were their last new AEC double-deckers.

AEC initially continued the prewar Regal and Regent. Regals supplied from the 1943 order were 18 with Saunders Engineering bodies in 1946, 18 with Brush bodies in 1947 and, for SDO, eight with the postwar BEF-standard 32-seat body built by Strachans in 1948. The best of these were the Brush-bodied versions — pleasant and lively 36-seaters allocated to the 'lowland' fleets, particularly Sunderland and South Shields depots. The Saunders bodies were unsatisfactory, all being sent back to Beaumaris for rebuilding and then having to be rebuilt again by Northern with strengthened bulkhead and pillars. Ten Regents (1167-76) were light, lively but noisy and were used to double-deck the 57 Sunderland–Durham service in September 1946 from Sunderland depot. At the end of 1946 Northern contributed to the cost of providing pavements to the Tyne Dock arches, thus allowing double-deckers to operate some of the South Shields services to Newcastle which the Regents also worked. SDO received 10 Roe-bodied Titan PD1s in 1946/7 to work the 57. Tyneside also got Titans — three PD1s with Leyland-designed Alexander

bodies (the Group's first from the Scottish builder, and the prelude to many more) and three all-Leyland PD2s in 1948 (the first in the Group).

After the PD1s, SDO got 11 Brush/BEF 32-seat Tiger PS1s in 1948 and its first-ever all-new coaches, two PS1/Duple 30-seaters, with four more in 1950. The last 'blue bus' vertical-engined single-deckers were the only PS2 Tigers bought by the Group — six with Roe/BEF bodies, which made light of the Sunderland–Consett services but which as 32-seaters soon became outmoded.

The new standard Guy single-deckers repeated the 1939 Regal formula, with very similar BEF-derived Brush 38-seat bodies. There were 50 in 1947, 50 in 1949 and 34 in 1950. Unlike the lighter Regals, they were not used at Stanley and Consett until very late in their lives, and, as with the postwar Guy double-deckers, each successive batch appeared to be more refined. The bodies of the 1947 and 1949 batches suffered from wood deterioration and had to be rebuilt, but these Guys still seemed to epitomise Northern's postwar fleet.

Gardner 5LW-powered Guy Arab III models with NCB 56-seat bodywork gradually dominated the double-deck fleet and its increasing use on longer services. Ten were delivered in 1946 and a further 10 in 1947. The latter batch was initially allocated

▲ SDO's AEC Regals of 1948 were an unusual batch, believed to be the only AECs fitted new with the postwar BEF body, and featuring the only BEF bodies built by Strachans. Unloved as AECs in a mainly Leyland fleet, their rough riding gave rise to their 'square-wheels' epithet. Although lively in performance (hence their use on the West Hartlepool service) they saw less-regular use after this was double-decked; three went to Tynemouth in red and cream as S193/4/6, while others worked on hire to Northern. *R. L. Kell*

to Tynemouth, until new AECs arrived. There were 20 more Arab/NCB in 1948 and a final 10 7ft 6in-wide versions in 1949, this batch being particularly competent and pleasant buses. Tynemouth/Wakefield's also had 10 Arabs in 1949 but with Pickering metal-framed bodies and, briefly, Meadows engines. Almost completing the 'narrow' double-deck scene, SDO took 14 excellent Roe-bodied buses — eight AEC Regent IIIs and six

Leyland PD2/1s — in 1950. After withdrawal, most went to Northern, the AECs being its only Regent IIIs.

Major fleet refurbishments were also ordered. All the early AEC Regents that had not been rebodied in wartime received postwar NCB bodywork, except for three Tynemouth Regents which gained Pickering bodies. The Leyland TD5s of Northern and Tynemouth received new Eastern Coach Works rear-entrance bodies. Four-cylinder SOSs were progressively withdrawn, but most IM6s and some ONs were comprehensively rebuilt with AEC 6.6-litre engines and new bodies by Pickering to a utilitarian standard. More comfortable Pickering bodies were fitted to the 1934/5 Regals and some of the Regal IIs. A Tyneside Leyland TD3 was rebodied by Burlingham and sent to the NGT fleet (1287).

The big news of 1949 was, however, the hire and then purchase from Yorkshire Woollen District of 25 12-year-old Leyland Tiger TS7s with 32-seat Roe/BEF bodies and thus almost identical to the SDO TS7s. Authority was given to overhaul and rebody if necessary. However, the bodies were good enough to rebuild, retaining the original seats, and the work was given to a firm set up by Major Hayter himself — the Picktree

Coach & Engineering Co in Picktree Lane, Chester-le-Street, beside the NGT depot. The 'new' buses (1301-25) became very effective and hard-working. The following year, to the delight of enthusiasts, eight 1937/8 AEC Regents with Park Royal bodies arrived from the City of Oxford fleet. Also in 1949/50, most of the 1939/40 Regal 'utilities' required attention to the bodies. Some were rebuilt, but the majority received new, almost identical Pickering or Picktree bodies to an NGT design based on the 1946 'utility' Pickering body —

The six-cylinder SOSs had many miles in front of them postwar, but their bodies needed work after 12 or so years. No 1002 (an IM6) and 1043 (an ON) both returned from war service, being converted to diesel power with AEC 6.6-litre engines from Army tanks and sent to Pickering for new basic 'utility' design bodies. This scene is at the Cattle Market near Marlborough Crescent, where the 1831 offices, designed by John Dobson, architect of nearby Newcastle Central station, were in use as a bank when photographed in July 1953; the building has now been restored, but Marlborough Crescent bus station has been swept away. *R. L. Kell*

One of the surprises of 1950 was the purchase of eight City of Oxford 1937/8 Park Royal-bodied AEC Regents, possibly as cover for any vehicle shortages or delivery delays during the Gateshead tram/bus changeover. These comfortable 52-seaters rapidly became favourites with enthusiasts, particularly on the Consett–Durham service. No 1395 worked the longest time for Northern after being rebodied in 1952 with the postwar NCB body from the only SOS double-decker (No 593). It has even been fitted with a stencil box under the canopy, itself no doubt taken from a withdrawn SOS. The scene is the cobbled Park Lane in Sunderland, and the Regent is on a local to either Pennywell (front) or Grindon (side) — they weren't far apart. In the background a new NCB–bodied Guy Arab (1383) waits to depart for Washington and Newcastle. The advert for the 'Working Men's' building society now has an antique air about it in this 'inclusive' age. *R. Marshall*

very strange, when, at the same time, Guy Arabs were being delivered with Brush bodies almost identical to those being removed from the Regals!

In 1949 Dixon Bros of Lanchester sold its 'Witbank' bus fleet to Northern, which took in (and actually ran) old PLSC Lions originating with SDO, as well as some Bedfords. The Tow Law–Lanchester service was extended to Stanley and the delightful Consett–Lanchester–Durham semi-rural service converted to double-deck operation from Consett depot.

A surprise was the hire (in 1948) and then purchase (in 1949) of 25 Yorkshire Woollen District 1935/6 Leyland Tiger TS7s with Roe 32-seat BEF bodies and very similar to SDO's TS7s. These 12-year-old buses were refurbished at Picktree Coachworks in Chester-le-Street (although the comfortable prewar seats were retained), after which they were worked hard throughout the system. No 1307 stands at Marlborough Crescent on a short working of the joint Newcastle–Bishop Auckland service, surrounded by two Venture Daimlers with Willowbrook bodies and a 1939 Bristol L5G/ECW of United. *R. Marshall*

Both the original Gateshead motor-bus orders for tram replacements — 20 Guys in 1950 and 37 PD2s in 1951 — were split unevenly between 8ft and 7ft 6in widths, the narrower buses being for use over the High Level Bridge. This photograph of 'wide' Guy 11 at Matthewbank when quite new in chocolate and cream shows that it still had its 'Indian chief' radiator cap and illuminated fleetname box, neither of which would last long. Park Royal had not been a supplier to the Group. The batch would be transferred to the Northern fleet in 1959. Gateshead alone adopted the Newcastle Corporation indicator layout. *R. C. Davis*

The 1951 purchase of J. W. Hurst & Sons' service to Blaydon and Winlaton out of Marlborough Crescent brought in five Guy Arab single-deckers —naturally at home in the NGT fleet — and three prewar and two postwar 30ft-long Dennis Lancets. The Lancets all had Associated Coachbuilders (ACB) bodies built in Sunderland. For once, Northern was tolerant of these strangers, the first Dennises operated. The J10 Lancets were almost new, and all were kept for 5-6 years. No 1448 was a 1938 Lancet II and originally a Dennis demonstrator. The ACB body has high-back seats, making it a dual-purpose vehicle; the J10 behind, 1456, had 39 bus seats. Both are waiting to duplicate on the Newcastle limited-stop express. Coach drivers liked the Lancet, a lively machine with good handling, and thus a preferable option to the 5LW-powered Guys which were also used to provide duplicates. *Photobus*

State monopoly vs private monopoly

In 1947 the Labour Government was intent upon nationalisation of essential industries and brought forward the Transport Act 1947 setting up the British Transport Commission (BTC) to exercise control of acquisitions — the four major railway companies (and their shareholding in companies such as Northern), London Transport, inland waterways and some road haulage. Bus companies were not included, but, with the proposal for 'area schemes' and, probably, compulsory purchase of unwilling operators, a threat was implied. The Tilling Group, which included United, sold its bus operations to the BTC in September 1948. The first area scheme was for Northumberland and Durham — one of Labour's heartlands — but the proposals met opposition. Northern adopted a public 'anti-nationalisation' stance, but crucial was the antipathy to 'big government' approach through Area boards from the mainly socialist towns of the North East, which would lose control of municipal transport which was already 'in the hands of the people'. The impetus for area schemes was lost when the Conservatives came to power in 1951.

The BTC, of course, continued, offering inducements to independent operators which would sell voluntarily; three did — Darlington Triumph, ABC of Ferryhill and Express of Durham. Express's base and main operations were on the 'Northern' side of Durham, and the other two ran to Sunderland, Triumph having a depot there. The obvious solution would have been to place these operations with the BTC's United, but this would have risked further upheaval with Northern unless the Sunderland and Durham operations were handed over. This was clearly unpalatable, and the answer was to set up an independent BTC company — Durham District Services Ltd — which was managed by United. The letter but not the spirit of the agreement was observed.

1950-3 — the end of the trams and DIY again

In 1950 Gateshead & District gained a Parliamentary Bill to allow it to replace the tramway with buses (the proposed conversion to trolleybuses having failed), and the name changed to the Gateshead & District Omnibus Co. The trams were finally withdrawn in August 1951 — the last BET trams in Britain. Replacement buses arrived in 1950/1: 35 Guy Arabs with Park Royal, NCB or Brush bodywork and 33 all-Leyland PD2s. Both types included a mix of 7ft 6in- and 8ft-wide bodies, painted chocolate with two cream bands, and it was assumed that the narrow buses were for operation over the High Level Bridge. The joint services to Beacon Lough and Wrekenton involved a long climb up from the river and the PD2s interworked with Newcastle Corporation's excellent PD2s and AEC Regent IIIs.

J. W. Hurst & Sons of Winlaton was bought in 1951, along with 11 single-deckers. Hurst's had operated in the Blaydon/Winlaton area since the 1920s, with main service operating out of Marlborough Crescent. In 1953 Hunter's Bus Service of Great Lumley, with services to Chester-le-Street, was bought out; a Tiger PS1 coach (Northern's only example of this chassis) was kept for four years.

With increased vehicle size came increased weight, and Gordon Hayter was publicly dissatisfied with the first generation of underfloor-engined single-deckers, which he considered grossly overweight for British use. He was not alone in this, of course, and a large order from BET for Leyland Royal Tigers was greeted with dismay by those developing lighter alternatives. If Royal Tigers were 'allocated' by BET, then Hayter had the luxury of declining to order but allowing Ernest Mountain at SDO his Royal Tiger choice of 10 Brush/BEF buses in 1951, eight Roe buses in 1952 and two Duple Coronation Ambassador coaches in 1953. Hayter was, at least, partly right: the comfortable, heavy Royal Tigers proved to have overheating problems on the climb up to Consett and heavy brake lining wear on the way down.

Weight was also a concern in the double-deck fleet. The traditional bodies were stretching the unladen weight to near 8 tons, and the 5LW was struggling; the narrow and lighter 5LW Arab had coped reasonably well, aided by the practice of 'knocking out' (of gear) on downhill sections to increase speed and get some peace and quiet. Mr Hayter published an article in 1952 criticising excess weight but also calculating aerodynamic

power losses by double-deckers into a headwind and concluding that 'it is very dangerous to use a high-powered engine, as on a windy day most of the fuel consumed … will be used to get a few extra mph against a strong headwind'. But a 5LW Arab could not get to 40mph on an uphill gradient in calm conditions. The 1952 delivery of 5LW-engined, beautifully crafted, comfortable heavyweights, which topped 8 tons unladen, 30 by Weymann (10 for Tynemouth) and 20 by Park Royal, lost time on such services as the 57, which had three long climbs out of Sunderland which could be taken in top or third gear with a PD2 or Regent III, third in a narrow Guy but a laden heavy Guy was down to second gear in places. Back came the lively lightweight 1946 Regents, and the Weymann and Park Royal Guys pottered around reliably on town services. A 6LW engine would have transformed them.

The reaction was draconian. The 1953 Arab IVs (30 for Northern, four for Tynemouth) with ultra-lightweight Weymann Aurora 58-seat bodies knocked off 1¼ tons, with thin, uncomfortable seats and extreme levels of noise and vibration. The following 31 (and five Tynemouth) Metro-Cammell Orion 63-seaters included 16 with platform doors for the inter-urban joint services. Middlesbrough to Newcastle on an Orion Arab with cramped seating was never to be forgotten. Something had to be done. In 1951 Northern had bought five all-Leyland PD2s 'at a favourable price', and Tyneside also had seven. With the

◀

This scene at South Shields encapsulates Northern's postwar fleet. No 1416 was a heavyweight 8ft-wide Guy Arab 5LW with RT-style Park Royal body of 1952. At almost 8 tons unladen, these comfortable buses were distressingly slow on any long uphill gradient, with consequential time loss. Behind 1416, a 38-seater Guy peeps out.

The 1947 Brush-bodied AEC Regals, such as 1151, were remnants of a large batch ordered from AEC during the war and the Group's happiest postwar Regals. These 36-seaters were particularly associated with South Shields depot until transferred to Stanley to replace prewar Regals. The 16 and 24 services both went to Newcastle, the 16 via Tyne Dock and Primrose and the 24 via Jarrow.
R. Marshall

Simply the best. In 1952 four Gateshead All-Leyland PD2/3s (46-9) were loaned to Northern, painted in red and cream, and then purchased and numbered in the Northern fleet (1479-82). When deployed on the 14 (South Shields–South Hetton) service, these buses were a revelation. Freed from town traffic, these early Leyland-bodied PD2s were in their element, quietly and powerfully dealing with any gradient or loading with ease, and the best of all PD2s. CCN 148 is seen in 1952 still carrying its Gateshead number. The South Hetton and Durham services terminated in Union Street, beside Sunderland station. On the right, Sunderland's new Binns store (of 'Shop at' fame) is being built to replace the bomb-damaged original. *R. Marshall*

The unwillingness to purchase heavyweight chassis in the early 1950s extended to coaches, except for Mr Mountain's two Leyland Royal Tigers with Duple Coronation Ambassador bodies at SDO. From 1951 to 1953, apart from 18 Beadle-AECs, there were 24 NGT-AECs designed by Major Hayter and his staff and built by Picktree Coachworks to two styles. Nos 1388 and 1368-76 were to the earlier style. None had bulkheads (nor did most of the Beadles), so the coaches were rather noisy with the AEC 7.7-litre engine under a cover at the front. *Go North East*

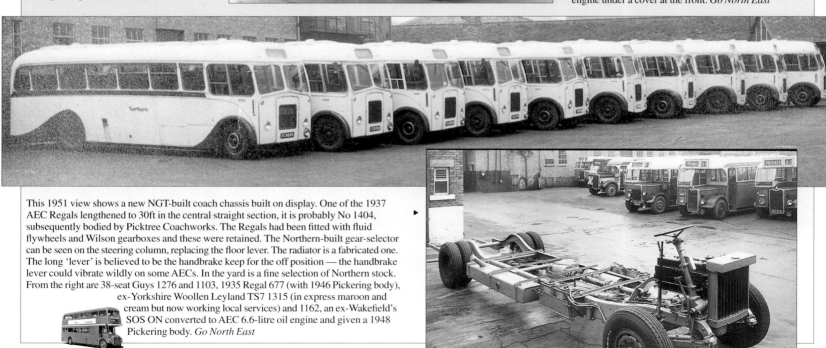

This 1951 view shows a new NGT-built coach chassis built on display. One of the 1937 AEC Regals lengthened to 30ft in the central straight section, it is probably No 1404, subsequently bodied by Picktree Coachworks. The Regals had been fitted with fluid flywheels and Wilson gearboxes and these were retained. The Northern-built gear-selector can be seen on the steering column, replacing the floor lever. The radiator is a fabricated one. The long 'lever' is believed to be the handbrake keep for the off position — the handbrake lever could vibrate wildly on some AECs. In the yard is a fine selection of Northern stock. From the right are 38-seat Guys 1276 and 1103, 1935 Regal 677 (with 1946 Pickering body), ex-Yorkshire Woollen Leyland TS7 1315 (in express maroon and cream but now working local services) and 1162, an ex-Wakefield's SOS ON converted to AEC 6.6-litre oil engine and given a 1948 Pickering body. *Go North East*

four ex-Gateshead PD2s, Northern actually had the nucleus of a smooth and quiet longer-distance fleet.

In 1951 NGT needed new stock while waiting for the new lightweight single-deck chassis to be developed. Spurning 30ft-long Arabs (which were heavy enough in 27ft 6in form) and apparently ignoring the BMMO S10, Mr Hayter turned to his trusty, reliable AEC Regal. The relatively light 1937 chassis could be lengthened to 30ft and new bodies fitted, 24 such vehicles being produced from 1951 to 1953 and bodied by Picktree Coachworks.

So impressed had the Company been with the 1920s SOS that the 'big single-decker' problem was temporarily solved by building what was unashamedly a 1951 QL. A straight-frame chassis to maximum dimensions was manufactured, to which was fitted a 7.7-litre AEC engine and manual transmission. The plain-sided, single-skin, arched-roof bodywork (without luggage racks) with 43 basic seats was built by Picktree. The complete bus weighed 6 tons 2cwt unladen and gave a better fuel consumption (14mpg) than the 38-seat Guys. The 12 production examples of 1953 (1467-78) had reasonable lives of nine years and endeared (if that is the correct word) themselves to all.

Finally the Group bought 18 Beadle integral coaches for Northern and Wakefield's which again used the 1937 Regal as the mechanical basis.

1954 — a year of change

The retirement of Gordon Hayter OBE and of Ernest Mountain at Sunderland District marked 1954 as a watershed 40th year for the Group. The new General Manager, James Forster, was a 'Northern' man through and through. He had started in the Company in 1922 — the same year as Major Hayter — and worked his way up through Traffic Superintendent to assistant to John Petrie, to Traffic Manager at Lincolnshire Road Car, back to Northern as Traffic Manager and then to General Manager at Trent. From 1955 until his retirement at the end of 1968, the company would be in firm and knowledgeable hands. Sunderland District's individuality became less marked, although the

identities of all the associated companies were maintained, and Northern's engineering expertise under L. M. Parker was devoted to general fleet matters rather than individual project design (for a time).

The evolution of the Leyland Tiger Cub, AEC/Park Royal Monocoach and Guy Arab LUF had now resulted in practical lightweight single-deckers. The 1954/5 intake was huge: 71 Tiger Cubs — of which 16 were for SDO — and 25 Monocoaches, all 44-seaters. Of these, the pick were the 31 Saunders-Roe Tiger Cubs, some with Eaton two-speed axles, and the Monocoaches, which gave good service from Stanley and Consett depots. Many more Weymann Hermes bodies were to follow the 40 on Tiger Cubs.

There was benefit to traffic and engineering from the new stock, but, by sweeping away most of the prewar fleet, they changed the character of the Company's operations. Most SOSs, prewar Leyland Tigers, SE buses and coaches and older AEC Regals met their end. Thereafter Northern was to work towards a vehicle life of 12 years, and the variety of vehicles rapidly declined. One event of historical importance occurred, however. John Birks, Assistant Traffic Manager (and later General Manager of Midland Red) spotted the two-axle SE6 bus, 604, in the 'scrap line' at Gateshead. Recognising its historical significance as the first modern underfloor-engined single-decker and the first 30ft-long two-axle one (since the 1920s experiments), he suggested that it be retained. It was duly presented by Gordon Hayter to John H. Scholes, the BTC's Curator of Historical Relics, and in 1955 it was driven down to the BTC Museum at Clapham, London.

▲ Massive orders for lightweight Leyland Tiger Cubs and AEC Monocoaches for 1954 spelt the end for most prewar machines. Some of the newcomers made a good impression, none more so than the Saunders-Roe-bodied Tiger Cubs. With small engines and slow gearbox, they gave reasonable (if not sparkling) performance only through their lightness. Those with two-speed axles were better on hills, but the ability of some drivers to make completely clutchless changes was a skill much admired. SDO individuality is still evident on nominally identical buses: No 269 is still lined-out, and fitted with drop (rather than sliding) ventilators. It and Northern 1550 are seen parked at Manors, Newcastle.
R. L. Kell

8. Gordon Hayter OBE in Retrospect

G. W. Hayter in 1932.
Go North East

Gordon Hayter was such a dominant figure within the Group and wrote so prolifically for the trade press, expressing sometimes controversial, sometimes far-sighted views, that he no doubt ruffled feathers. But was he an influential national figure?

He became an expert sorter-out of vehicles, curing major faults in design and construction with the aim of producing maximum-capacity practical and reliable vehicles which had long life and low running costs. Passenger comfort in service was secondary to reliability and safe, economical travel, but long-distance and tour passengers were treated to the finest contemporary vehicles.

The sorting-out included the Daimler/AEC Y type, the Leyland Lion PLSC (which needed little mechanical improvement, other than to the brakes) and AEC Reliances (1920s) and Regals, particularly the Regal II. He was not in the vanguard of early oil-engine development or of the use of double-deckers, both of which he regarded with some scepticism. His public contrast between 1928 SOS QL (at 3¾ tons and 8mpg on petrol) and 1950 Guy Arab (at 6¾ tons and 11mpg on diesel) over the same routes questioned how much had really changed, as both had similar seating capacity. His scepticism of the oil engine was that its weight and high torque at low speed meant that a much more robust and heavier transmission was needed, requiring heavier frames, while high front-axle loadings led to heavy steering, and much of the inherent economy of the oil engine was surrendered. His admired Wyndham Shire at Midland Red did not rush to build oil engines and, when he did, produced notably compact ones.

Hayter's reputation as an innovator relies principally upon the SE buses and coaches of 1933 to 1939. Some may consider the SE a derivative of G. J. Rackham's AEC Q, and its completion was some months behind that of Q1. Hayter, however, writing in 1935 (perhaps to counter comment that it was derivative), clearly stated that 'by an extraordinary coincidence the Northern General SE6 and the A. E. Company's Q-type, presenting many features in common, were developed independently and almost simultaneously'. Hayter cited the Daimler KPL of 1910 as the true originator of the SE. Indeed, as he had served his time at Daimler, he was probably there when it was built. Although markedly different in some ways to the Q (front radiator, narrow chassis with differential outside, Hercules engine etc), the SE did infringe Q patents. In 1932, however, AEC had carried out

lengthy correspondence with the Twin Coach Corporation, Ohio, USA, over allegations that the Q designs infringed existing Twin Coach patents! It must also be remembered that NGT was bound to take longer to design and produce experimental chassis. AEC had design and drawing offices whereas Northern had not built a vehicle off the drawing board before, and the SE6, with the twin-axle bogie, was more complicated than the Q. It is also arguable that the SE was more influential than the Q single-decker. Donald Sinclair, apprenticed at Albion Motors, was interviewed as a 'designer' in 1935 and must have been in charge of much of the design work of the SE6. In 1940 he succeeded the great Wyndham Shire at BMMO, and the consequence of this was the first wholesale adoption by a major fleet of the front-facing-seat single-decker with driver-supervised entrance — the BMMO S6. The SE6 was, perhaps, in its limited way, a more successful vehicle than the Q, particularly the outstanding coach version. The SE was also commendably light — 6 tons 2cwt for the 40-seat SE4 'oiler' and 6½ tons for the SE6.

Hayter also remained broadly faithful to AEC products when that firm was going through a bad patch in the mid-1930s. The Q, Regal 4 and Regal II and the railcars had not been successful. The AEC sales team gave stinging criticism to the AEC Board in March 1937 in explaining their difficulties in selling AECs to fleets where Daimler and Leyland chassis were in use: '… the qualities of performance… by engines of Gardner and Leyland make together with the excellent chassis… it is almost impossible to dislodge them… the lamentable failure in service of the recent edition of the AEC oil engine…'.

In 1953 the chairmen of Northern General and Yorkshire Traction mounted an investigation into maintenance costs at NGT in comparison with YTC. Statistics from 1952 were used when NGT had 653 buses (not including the Group fleets) and YTC, which had greater double-deck mileage (40%, against 33% for NGT), 354. NGT had an older fleet, the average for chassis being 9.7 years (YTC 6.5) and for bodies 6.9 years (YTC 5.2). NGT did have much higher maintenance costs than YTC, but there were mitigating factors. Northern's fleet was much older (chassis replacement life 19 years (!) — YTC 13 years) but this was at a time when Hayter was holding off the purchase of new single-deckers until the new lightweight designs were available. This low depreciation at Northern reduced effective maintenance costs from 0.75d per car mile to 0.48, which was still higher than YTC's. In defence, Northern cited its hillier services in a poorer climate and the 'exacting nature of the MoT Certifying Officer for the North East (formerly the manager of a team of racing cars!)'. He 'insisted on an annual inspection of every bus, the unnecessary replacement of mechanical units and generally adopted an uncompromising attitude'. The NGT fleet was very reliable despite its age; the author never saw a broken-down Group bus in all his years of daily travel — until the 1960s! The lower costs at YTC were judged to be due to its central works, where all docking was carried out. Hayter's 1924 system at NGT made individual garages responsible for maintenance — Chester-le-Street (256 buses, including those based at Sunderland and Murton), Stanley (147, including Consett), Bensham (164, including Hurst's) and South Shields (89). The other companies looked after themselves.

Gordon Hayter's comments were that contemporary (heavy-weight) underfloor-engined chassis had grave disadvantages in high first cost and in cost of operation; investment in new lightweight chassis would make considerable savings. He also noted that (his) SE4 and SE6 chassis had the lowest brake-lining wear in the fleet.

While perhaps not in the first rank of passenger-transport engineers, such as L. G. Wyndham Shire and G. J. Rackham, Gordon Hayter was most definitely in the second rank — his SE series of buses and coaches being at the peak of 1930s craftsman-ship and design — and influential through BMMO. His retirement in 1954 led to consultancy (with Linjebuss in Sweden), writing and a Directorship of Guy Motors, but he was to survive only for three years.

James Forster took over at a time of maximum ownership and ridership of the Group's buses, the fleet peaking at 989 in 1956. His leadership of a largely settled system was to maximise income from the dense network of services provided principally within an area of around 600 square miles which included the municipal operations of Newcastle, Sunderland and South Shields and vigorous independent operators at the edges (Venture Transport, OK Motor Services, Economic and Trimdon Motor Services) and was surrounded by the nationalised United Automobile Services and Durham District Services. The Group had always respected and worked with tradition in allowing managership and a degree of independence among its associated companies. While James Forster took over as General Manager at Sunderland District upon the retirement of Ernest Mountain, Gateshead & District, even though only a mile or so from Northern's Head Office at Bensham, continued under the management of J. W. King until his retirement in 1963. Philadelphia, Sunderland Road and Percy Main also handled their own maintenance and overhaul of buses and were thus semi-independent, with their own engineers.

One major initiative was the very successful introduction of local express services duplicating stage services. It was known that some services between major towns carried many through passengers, and, to retain these, in competition with train and car, hourly services with only one or two stops, in coaches with special blue/yellow blinds, started in September 1959: X1 (Newcastle–Durham), X2 (Newcastle–South Shields), X3 (Sunderland–Durham) and X4 (Sunderland–Newcastle). These were supplemented by the X6 (Sunderland–Consett) in 1961, when Saturday frequencies were increased. The X7 (Newcastle–Blaydon–Winlaton) was introduced in 1965 and the X5 (Newcastle–West Hartlepool with SDO and United) in 1966 on a new route through Washington and Houghton. Originally coaches were supplemented by express buses, but the image would later suffer when ordinary buses and double-deckers participated.

The Group was late to adopt one-person operation of buses, probably because of the dense and smartly-timed nature of its operations, but a start was made in 1967 with Murton's Houghton-le-Spring–Seaham service and thereafter spread to quieter Consett and SDO operations.

The opening of the Tyne Tunnel between Jarrow and Howden

in 1967 allowed cross-Tyne services in the east. The Sunderland–Jarrow service (60) was extended to Blyth and run jointly with Tynemouth and United, and a joint Hebburn–Cramlington service also started. There now remained few operators which did not wish to continue, so only minor competition was purchased —J. & T. Hunter (Washington) Ltd's Usworth Colliery–Waterside (River Wear!) local operation in 1963.

The structures of the statutory Gateshead and Tyneside companies changed in 1965 to incorporate limited liability, after which the Tyneside Tramways & Tramroads Co Ltd changed again almost immediately to become the Tyneside Omnibus Co Ltd.

This period also saw major property developments, starting with Chester-le-Street. For many years Northern had out-parked most of its fleet behind the depot beside the A167 by-pass, but a major development saw the garage's capacity increase from 70 buses to 167. In 1956 a new Company bus station was built at Park Lane, Sunderland, with a new 55-bus garage beside it. There was also a new Winlaton depot in 1957. In 1958/9 Philadelphia gained a major 40-bus extension (as did Percy Main) and the old coach house and tramway offices were demolished in favour of a new office block. Murton gained an extension for 23 buses and Jarrow was next, with a new depot in 1961 beside the bus station opened in 1954. Bensham was extended and modernised in 1962, the new paint shop replacing the old Cullercoats property of Tynemouth. In 1965 Tyneside vacated the leased ex-tram depot at Neptune Bank for a purpose-built garage at Hadrian Road, Wallsend.

Vehicles

With the advent of the practical lightweight bus, for the first time since 1922 Northern-designed or -modified vehicles were not needed, and fleet replacements proved to be much more akin to BET Group practice than previously (and were consequently much less interesting!). New single-deckers were almost confined to Northern and SDO, although double-deckers increased their representation there. The Tynemouth fleet was almost entirely double-deck in BET days, and Gateshead and Tyneside completely so.

The period started with two oddities. Nos 1625/6 were Beadle-Commer TS3 underfloor-engined single-deckers. The author

NORTHERN
GENERAL TRANSPORT COMPANY LTD

INTER ⚡ URBAN

EXPRESS SERVICES

X.1 Newcastle Chester-le-Street Durham

X.2 Newcastle – – South Shields

X.3 Durham Houghton-le-Spring Sunderland

X.4 Newcastle – – Sunderland

Starting on
SATURDAY, 5th SEPTEMBER, 1959

Timetables overleaf · Fares and conditions on back page

Travel by Bus!

▲ Leaflet introducing Northern's innovative inter-urban express services, X1–X4, September 1959. *R. L. Kell collection*

rode on the Consett service to try one: unfortunately it was driven as if it was a conventional diesel with good low-speed torque. The TS3 died under this treatment — it needed to be revved for power, whereupon it would go well, sounding like a demented wasp. They were judged a failure and after four years were sold to Charlton's of Hexham to potter successfully around Northumberland lanes.

Guys were still in favour in 1955 — 22 Arab LUF single-deckers with five-speed gearboxes — while the intake of MCW Orion-bodied double-deckers included two for Gateshead and five for Tynemouth. SDO got five Tiger Cubs to see off the last prewar Tigers. The last Guys — 20 (plus eight for Tynemouth) passenger-friendly Park Royal-bodied Arab IVs — were delivered in 1956.

It was now over to Leyland for all double-deckers until 1964. More Titan PD2s arrived — the five Orion 'bouncers' for SDO, 10 fast but cramped Park Royal 63-seaters to upgrade the long-distance services and three Willowbrooks for Tynemouth. Thereafter it was Titan PD3s with Orion bodies for 1958 (five for Gateshead, three for Tyneside, 12 for Tynemouth/Wakefield's and 20 for Northern), plus the Burlingham-bodied batch of 13 (with

doors) for SDO. That was the end of the front-engined double-decker, we thought.

Leyland's new, rear-engined Atlantean seated 77 or 78, which impressed the traffic staff, so the Group invested heavily, and the

45

BET was reportedly unhappy with Northern's adherence to Guy Motors on the grounds of initial chassis cost, and after 1956 the Company changed to Leyland and AEC. The 28 Guy Arab IVs of 1956 retrieved Guy's reputation. Their light Park Royal bodies were a cut above the previous Orions, with better internal finish and quieter travel, but as 5LW-engined 63-seaters they were strictly for shorter bus services. Here 1697-1702 are lined up ready for delivery near Wolverhampton in the 1956 'cream top' colours. The eight Tynemouth examples (less one written off) later joined the NGT fleet. *Ian Allan Library*

Twelve PDR1 Atlanteans were delivered in 1961 as standard 77-seaters with Roe bodywork. All were in red with single cream band, and a number worked out of Murton depot, where 1965 is seen when new. The destination and service number are very appropriate: Northern's first double-deckers in 1931 worked out of Murton, and the 123 to Dawdon (then 23) was one of the first double-deck services from Sunderland. *Go North East*

The 1919 fleet-numbering system had almost reached 2000 when the 1962 block system was introduced, with double-deckers starting from 2001. The 10 1966 Leyland Atlanteans with Alexander bodies were thus 2135-44. Delivered in all red, three are posed when new at the Tyne Commission Quay on the north bank of the Tyne, near North Shields. The Group has long held contracts to carry foot passengers to Newcastle Central station, and Tynemouth, Tyneside, Gateshead and Northern buses were used at times. With the ships travelling mainly to Norway and Denmark, there was good business from Scandinavian shoppers. *Go North East*

type was to dominate the double-deck fleet until the end of the model. Ten Alexander-bodied PDR1s for Gateshead in 1959 started the rush, and thereafter GDO bought another 43 up to 1968. Northern took 117 from 1960 to 1968, and SDO 19. Tyneside started late, with 10 from 1964 to 1968. Tynemouth also started with Atlanteans, with 22 in 1962, but suggestions from BET that the Daimler Fleetline offered better fuel economy led it to buy 35 between 1963 and 1968. Early bodywork was mainly by the MCW group and Roe, but from 1964 the choice was Alexander, whose body now became the NGT Group standard. The Alexander Atlantean was *the* area bus of the 1960s.

By 1963/4 doubts were beginning to creep in over the new generation of rear-engined double-deckers — the steel-framed bodies (particularly from Roe) were starting to show serious corrosion, the chassis were more open to driver abuse, with heavy maintenance costs and lower reliability, and were they the most comfortable vehicles for the longer-distance inter-urban joint services? Northern's answer was to order 50 AEC/Park Royal Routemasters to its own specification — 30ft-long, forward-entrance, with Leyland engine, and some with interiors to the Reid Consultancy's design brief. The extra initial

cost would be recouped by reduced maintenance costs resulting in part from improved corrosion resistance, and so it proved, the 50 Routemasters (plus the experimental RMF1254 re-engined with a Leyland) of 1964/5 becoming the flagships of the double-deck fleet.

There were two major livery changes. Gateshead's 1964 Alexander-bodied Atlanteans introduced Tyneside-style green

The 1959 single-deckers were all-red. Willowbrook got that year's order for 28 45-seat buses — 20 Leyland Tiger Cubs and eight AEC Reliances. Tiger Cub 1888, still quite new when photographed under the South Shields trolleybus wires in October of that year, is passing 1754, also a Willowbrook-bodied Tiger Cub but in this case a 'coach'. The 18 urban service from South Shields was one of the few that terminated at Wellington Street bus station in Gateshead rather than continuing to Newcastle. This busy location, at Slake Terrace, Tyne Dock, has now been redeveloped out of existence. *D. F. Parker*

and cream to replace the old chocolate, which looked dowdy on these bigger buses. The Tynemouth fleet received a welcome lift in 1966 when it reverted to the 1940s livery of red with cream window surrounds and roof. This certainly brightened up Wallsend on a wet day, and it spread partly to Northern also, some RMs and Alexander double-deckers being painted thus.

Single-deckers now included many more coach-seated buses, as the image of the bus fleet also improved. For 1956/7, as well as express-coach Reliances (15) and Tiger Cubs (10) bodied by Willowbrook, Northern took in 16 Reliance and 20 Tiger Cub 44-seaters, plus five lightweight Albion Aberdonians, all with Weymann bodies. Tynemouth also had two Reliance/Willowbrook DPs. The 34 Burlingham-bodied Reliances of 1958 were a cut above the Weymanns in terms of internal finish and seating, even if 45-seaters. They were also very smart in red and cream but sadly the last in this livery, as the 38 Willowbrook Reliances and Tiger Cubs of 1959 were in unrelieved red.

The only single-deckers in 1960 were two Metro-Cammell coach-seated Tiger Cubs for SDO. The 1961 deliveries were a batch of hard-worked Alexander 41-seat Reliances in dual-purpose colours, while SDO got three buses and two DPs — all Alexander-bodied Tiger Cubs.

The first 36ft-long buses and first Leopard buses were 10 with Willowbrook 53-seat BET bodies for Stanley (plus two DP versions for Wakefield's), followed by 19 similarly bodied Reliances in 1963. SDO, meanwhile, started a run of 37 BET-style 36ft Leopards up to 1968 to modernise the fleet. Tynemouth had two Leopard/Willowbrook buses. For the final three years under BET, Northern reverted to Leopards, with 30 Marshall-bodied examples (15 buses and 15 DPs) in 1966, 12 more Marshall DPs in 1967 and 12 Willowbrook DPs in 1968, the amount of cream increasing on the later DP vehicles. There was another sign that single-deck orders would become more innovative when a Leopard arrived with a strikingly modern

body by Marshall, named the Camair. This came to Winlaton depot as a bus, 2332, although it didn't look like it, with its cream-and-red livery.

The coaching stock was mainly (but not entirely) first-class but varied in supplier even more than did the buses. They could be divided into Continental/home tourers (all top-quality) and day-tour coaches (sometimes in bus-type shells), of which the latter could be usefully demoted to express and local-tour work after a few years.

The period started well, with six Weymann Fanfares for Wakefield's on AEC Reliance chassis, as well as the 10 Guys for Northern, but the 1957 Willowbrook-bodied Tiger Cubs were a let-down. SDO had two unusual Park Royal 'Royalist' coaches on Reliance chassis (its only Reliances) and two Tiger Cub/Duple Donington coaches in 1958 (later to be downgraded). Northern

bought 10 Willowbrook Viking coaches on Reliance in 1959 which were later rebuilt as useful DPs for express work. Harrington Cavaliers were an excellent choice in 1960 (10 Reliance) and 1961 (10 Leopard L2), the latter replacing the 1954 Guys on Continental tours. SDO also got two Burlingham-bodied Tiger Cubs in 1961, to work Northern extended tours.

The next intake was in 1963 and a surprise — short-life Bedfords. Eight, bodied by Harrington, were for Northern and two each, by Plaxton, for SDO and Wakefield's. The same year the first 36ft-long coaches were bought — five 44-seat Leopard/ Harrington Grenadiers for Continental work and five 49-seat Reliance/Plaxtons for home tours. SDO got two 36ft Leopards with Plaxton bodies in 1966. The last coaches of the BET era were 10 Alexander Y-types on Leopard chassis, of which two were for Wakefield's.

▲ Northern's 1933 Tours programme depicts an idyllic Britain viewed from an open (but with sliding canvas roof) SOS QLC coach. *R. L. Kell collection*

▲ Northern/Ribble Newcastle–Blackpool timetable, 1936. *R. L. Kell collection*

10. Coaching and Long-distance Express

After the 1914-18 war, with its rapid development of the petrol-engined lorry, open-topped or -sided bodies were fitted for passenger trips when the chassis would otherwise have been idle. These developed into the purpose-built charabanc, mainly on Daimler, Thornycroft and Leyland chassis operated by such pioneers as Thomas Wakefield of North Shields or Pomeroys of Craghead, Durham. Northern moved into excursions and tours with six Latymer-bodied 'charas' (D31-6) on Daimler Y-type chassis in 1920. Motor travel could take parties further than the horse-brake, and even exposure to wind, cold, rain and the risk of breakdown didn't dampen the sense of adventure.

With increased confidence in the vehicles, in 1922 NGT started scheduled seven-day tours of Scotland, for which the bodies were mounted on newer chassis converted to pneumatic tyres for the 1925 season. Side screens could be erected to fit between the door and sliding canvas roof when needed. However, even for the hardy 1920s, if the weather was 'wet or threatening', 20-seater Daimler 'saloon buses' would be substituted. Extended tours were now to the Lake District as well as Scotland.

In 1927 the fleet was supplemented by six SOS QC open coaches (ex-BMMO) and two- and three-day tours to Blackpool were changed to a daily coach trip which evolved into an express service from Newcastle via Kirby Stephen and Lancaster. The extended tours, presumably now by SOS, were of 3, 4, 5, 7, 8, 10 and 14 days' duration. Two more QCs and 10 QLC all-weather coaches ('Hail, Rain or Shine, Comfort all the Time', as the advertisement went) in 1928 brought the extended tours entirely into SOS hands, starting from the new coach station in Westgate Road, Newcastle. The 14-day tour, staying in first-class hotels, cost £22. The touring programme was changed from year to year, but the 10- and 14-day tours were eventually dropped.

The success of the daily Blackpool trip led to the introduction of daily coach services to Keswick (via Hexham, Alston and Penrith) and to Liverpool (via Leeds, Oldham and Manchester). Various independent operators had pioneered Leeds and Liverpool services, but Northern was the first 'company' operator, albeit initially for through traffic only. In May 1929 the trip had become a two-hourly stopping service with SOS Madam buses; worked jointly with North Western Road Car, West Yorkshire Road Car and Yorkshire (Woollen District) Electric Tramways, this was the foundation of the 'Limited Stop' pool for distributing receipts. A new limited-stop service was also run to Southport. Northern's first enclosed and half-cab coaches (10 SOS SRR models) were purchased in 1930 especially for these services.

Northern advertised a Newcastle–Birmingham service in 1932, but this involved changing at Leeds and presaged the purchase in March 1933 of the Fawdon Bus Co, initially a local Newcastle operator which had developed a Newcastle–Birmingham/Coventry service, as many North Easterners had moved to the Midlands to work in the motor industry. The Fawdon registered office remained in Newcastle (or at NGT at Bensham), but the ownership was a joint one of West Yorkshire, Northern, East Yorkshire, North Western, Yorkshire Traction and Yorkshire Woollen District, with mainly the latter's coaches being used. The Liverpool service was now officially 'Limited Stop' and the Blackpool and Keswick services were operated jointly with Ribble Motor Services. Further purchases in 1933 by the group of operators were independent competitors Leeds & Newcastle Omnibus Co and Tyne & Mersey Motor Services.

Three 14-seat Commer Centaurs were bought in 1934 for the Scottish tours, but the real sensation was the arrival of the

The author contends that the SE6 coaches of 1935 and 1936 were the most advanced and impressive tourers of the 1930s, and indeed, into the 1950s with 2+1 armchair seating for 28 in a 30ft-long vehicle. They retained their American Hercules WXC3 383cu in (6.7-litre) petrol engines to the last, being withdrawn only after the 1954 season. No 652 was photographed in 1946 after preparation for the resumption of postwar touring. These superb coaches — Nos 651-6 (with Short Bros bodywork) and 727/8 (Beadle) — were the flagships of NGT chassis production. Was armchair travel ever more luxurious?
Go North East

magnificent SE6 coaches with Short Bros coachwork and 2+1 seating for the 1935 season. Except for the war years, these vehicles, supplemented by two more in 1936, were the principal coaches for the longer extended tours until 1954, illustrating their advanced design and pre-eminence in comfort, and were driven by selected crews from Chester-le-Street depot. They took a few years to assume their final form, having evolved from open-roof coaches with fixed side windows and front and rear domes into metal-roof (with sliding section) coaches with glazed cantrail windows and shapely luggage pod on the roof.

Further old SOS QC and QLC coaches were bought from BMMO in 1935, as many of the QLCs were used by Wakefield's for touring and hire from Whitley Bay. Three Charlton's Leyland-bodied Tiger TS1 'buses' (which had run the South Shields–London service) were rebodied in 1938 with the superb Duple Coronation body to work Keswick expresses and would be converted to oil engines in 1952. The 1938/9 deliveries of these bodies on new AEC Regal and Leyland Tiger TS8 chassis for both Northern and Wakefield's meant that these coaches handled

some extended tours, most day tours and hires, and, later, express services until 1954. The express services got ten Brush coaches on TS8 chassis in 1938.

Despite the acquisitions, the number of coaches was insufficient to meet all the summer demands. Supplementary vehicles were needed, and there is some photographic evidence that the 'best buses' used for such work were the SOS M, IM6 and ON types. In some, at least, a rear seat was removed and luggage racking installed, and these also had suitable head or side running boards or roller blinds. Some of the 1936 AEC Regal II and 1937 pre-selector Regal buses were fitted with half-length ceiling racks and could thus be used as relief 'coaches'.

Extended and day touring and, eventually, express services ceased after the outbreak of war, and many of the coaches were laid up. They resumed in 1946 with the comfortable prewar SE6s, Tigers and Regals. The great demand for coach and express travel found Northern — and other companies — wanting in the provision of suitable duplicating vehicles. Between 1939 and 1951 there were only the prewar coaches, supplemented by 10 1949 Guys with Windover bodies, or utilitarian buses. Duplication of the 10 1938 TS8 express coaches was often with 38-seat prewar AEC Regal or postwar Guy Arab — hardly the best way to treat the customer, hence the extraordinary use of the 15-year-old Yorkshire Woollen TS7s before the purpose-built express-coach AEC Reliances arrived in 1956.

By 1950 Northern was offering tours of up to 10 days, stay-at-home tours, day and half-day and mystery and evening tours from 24 towns and villages, and, as the brochure said, 'Northern Luxury Holiday Tours enmesh the face of our country and weave a wonderful web of road romance'. And the vehicles? 'The modern touring coaches, specially designed, will take you in luxurious comfort and effortless ease…'. The 'modern touring coaches' were 15 years old and still ahead of any competitor and most of what was on offer from the commercial manufacturers at the time, which reveals their outstanding conception and design.

In 1951 Continental tours were added by arrangement with Sheffield United Tours. Passengers could travel to Sheffield by the Fawdon–Birmingham express and stay overnight or, to save a day each way, join at Dover. In 1954 Northern supplemented these tours with its own, via the Channel ports to France and Switzerland, via sea to Denmark and on to Germany and the Low Countries or via sea to Norway. New coaches (to replace the faithful SE6s) were needed for this venture, and 13 Gardner 6HLW-powered Guy Arab LUFs were the choice, with bodies designed and built at Picktree Coachworks.

Also in 1954, Northern purchased Bee-Line Continental Tours Ltd of Newcastle (but no vehicles), and this firm handled the foreign tours until 1957, when it was wound up.

Air-coach Continental tours quickly developed for 1957, with passengers flying from Woolsington Airport (as it then was) to pick up either an outstationed Northern coach or one from a local operator. These were dropped in 1958 and replaced by SUT air-coach tours, Northern passengers reaching Sheffield by train and then taking the coach to Ringway, Manchester. Coach-air holidays to the Isle of Man used the express to Blackpool and then plane to Douglas.

For 1961, Harrington Cavalier-bodied Leopards replaced the Guys on Continental work and were in turn replaced by long Leopard/Grenadiers in 1966. By 1968 many people, having had their first experience of flying (and of a European holiday) on a Northern tour were moving to 'package' tours to resorts in Spain.

The apparent anomaly of Northern's 12 SOS ON buses of 1934 (now at the longer permitted length of 27ft 6in) seating 34 (in a high-seating-capacity fleet) and Sunderland District's 10 seating 38 (in a low-seating-capacity fleet) is solved by this view of Northern 613 at Keswick. With no specific express or dual-purpose coaches in the fleet, the duplication and working of express services and day tours must have been handled by 'super' buses with reduced seating capacity. Six-cylinder petrol-engined SOS buses particularly undertook this work, being smoother, quieter, faster and more comfortable than many postwar oil-engined coaches. All Northern's ONs were requisitioned in 1940; although most returned, 613 did not, instead finding its way to Brookes Bros of Castle Gresley. *A. Cross*

▲ Among the excellent 1938 Leyland deliveries were 10 TS8s with Brush coach bodies for the Liverpool and Coventry express services. As well-equipped 30-seaters they were top-class vehicles which battered their way over the West Riding and Lancashire stone setts and tram tracks for most of their lives. When the express services came off during the war, they did not go into hibernation but were converted temporarily to buses with perimeter seating. Some lost their elegant roof-mounted luggage platforms in postwar rebuilding. No 866 and an unidentified sister are seen in Harrogate in what must be a prewar view, with the coaches carrying route boards. The low-mounted driving lights were a Northern characteristic. *The Omnibus Society*

The use of 15-year-old ex-Yorkshire Woollen District buses as scheduled express 'coaches' was remarkable in the early 1950s. At least five (1312/3/5/6/20) were painted in maroon-and-cream coach livery for the work, but that didn't stop many of the red-and-cream examples reaching Liverpool. While these vehicles were not luxuriously appointed, the 32 original seats all faced forward, were comfortable and had more room than Northern's newer buses. The old Tiger TS7 was a reasonably fast and smooth machine, and some operators were still fitting new bodies to these chassis at the time. The buses had also been overhauled and the bodies renovated. Still, the image is a little antiquated compared with the postwar coaches sharing (with pigs!) the Leeming halt in North Yorkshire.
R. Marshall

▲ The use of small petrol-engined coaches in the 1950s was unexpected, and one such, 1528, a Commer Commando with Plaxton coachwork, is seen leaving Wellington Street, Leeds, on a Newcastle express in July 1953. It is in all-red livery with, apparently, black wings. The many passengers would have quite a pleasant run. JUP 477 of 1948 came to NGT with the fleet of S. Hunter of Great Lumley in March 1953 together with a Lumley–Chester-le-Street service. *D. F. Parker*

▲ The first true express coaches were the 15 Willowbrook-bodied AEC Reliances of 1956 which went straight onto the long-distance limited-stop services. They were very capable go-anywhere vehicles. No 1719 heels over as it leaves Ripon bus station, with conductor on board, in July 1957. *D. F. Parker*

Most of the Northern and SUT holidays were now air-coach or simply a package visit to Spain or Majorca, with the holiday 'spent at leisure at the resort of choice', as the brochure put it.

The Fawdon Bus Co, nominally operating the Coventry service which allowed transfer to other coach networks from Birmingham to Cheltenham, was wound up in 1959, and the co-operating companies operated the service as the 'Ten Cities Express'. For 1966 a new overnight Friday- and Sunday-only express (X95) was started from Newcastle to Hanley. This shared the route of the Coventry service to Barnsley and then diverted via Buxton. Potteries Motor Traction joined the pool as operator with Northern, United, West Yorkshire, Yorkshire Woollen District, Yorkshire Traction, North Western and Lancashire United.

▲ Northern/Sheffield United Tours air-coach holidays leaflet, 1958. *R. L. Kell collection*

▲ For 1951— Festival of Britain year — NGT's Tours programme still featured the magnificent SE6 coaches of 1935. *R. L. Kell collection*

◄ Limited-stop Tyne–Tees–Mersey timetable, 1958. *R. L. Kell collection*

Concord bus station marked the centre of old Washington. A sunny November day in 1967 finds two Marshall-bodied Leyland Leopards departing. In unrelieved red, 53-seat bus version 2302 (in Northern's new block-allocated numbers — 2251 upwards were buses) heads for just-down-the-road Brady Square *en route* from Chester-le-Street. The well-laden dual-purpose 49-seater behind is almost certainly one of the 2509-23 batch (2501 upwards being DPs) and is Newcastle-bound on the 39 service from Murton.
R. L. Kell

11. The End of BET

In 1962 the BTC was wound up, and the newly created Transport Holding Co took over its bus operating businesses. In 1966, however, with Labour back in power, plans were floated for transport authorities in areas of high polution density — an idea which harked back to the 1940s. BET made a show of opposition, but Barbara Castle, Minister of Transport, was keen to develop integrated transport and saw BET's national network as an obstacle to this. The motor car and television had damaged ridership, and BET was in no mood to manage reducing services and declining profits. It entered into negotiations, eventually accepting £35 million for the transfer to the THC of its national bus interests from 1 March 1968, and the 1968 Transport Act made provision for the formation, from 1 January 1969, of the National Bus Company, to combine the former BET and THC groups. Northern's 'Glory Days' under BET had come to an end, but the next 20 years were to prove just as fascinating under NBC and with deregulation. But that must wait for another day.

Northern timetable cover
featuring NGT SE6 bus,
1951. *R. L. Kell collection*

Northern route map from
the 1951 timetable.
R. L. Kell collection

The 1947-50 Guy Arab 38-seaters followed the 1939/40 AEC Regals as the core stock of the postwar single-deck fleet, although, as they were much heavier than the Regals and thus relatively underpowered, they weren't the 'go-anywhere' buses that the Regals were. Despite this, they were well regarded and were characteristic North East vehicles. The Brush bodies were to a high-floor Northern design derived from the BEF body, but the GUP and KPT batches had to be re-pillared in the 1950s. The high build was then unfashionable, and a dozen or so were rebuilt with extended panelling. The result, as shown here, merely looked heavy. No 1076 has worked from Durham into Newcastle on the 46 in June 1958. *R. L. Kell*

In July 1958 Northern's oldest and only remaining prewar buses, the 1939/40 AEC Regal 'utility' 38-seaters, were all out of service, but a number, including 958 at Stanley, were awaiting disposal. These Regal Bs were mostly rebodied with almost identical Pickering (1949) and Picktree (1950) bodies to a Northern design brief which was a developed version of Pickering's 1946 body. No 958 had the Picktree version. The Regal B chassis dispensed with engine fans and frequently boiled up on warm days on the stiff climbs up to Stanley from Chester-le-Street and Gateshead. The buses would stop for a bucket of water at Stanley depot or at motor garages in the Whickham area or even from houses! *R. L. Kell*

Northern's postwar fleet of Northern Coachbuilders (of Newcastle) Guy Arabs dominated the new double-deck workings just as the Guy 38-seaters dominated the single-deck ones. There were 50 of them with 7ft 6in-wide bodies. No 1193 has had some pillar strengthening but is otherwise in good shape for its 10 years in May 1958. The new, simplified livery just introduced as an economy by James Forster dispensed with lining-out, black wings etc and looked good in the sunshine when new but dreary in the rain when the gloss had worn off. The bus is parked near the cattle market, but this whole area is now part of the 'Centre for Life' development.

R. L. Kell

▲ The first postwar coaches were 10 Meadows-engined Guy Arabs with handsome Windover coachwork. They were used to supplement the 1935 NGT SE6 coaches on week-long coach tours. Later they were used for express services but had relatively short (eight-year) lives. The Meadows engines gave a good performance but were eventually replaced with AEC 7.7-litre units to improve economy. By 1957, when Guy/Windover coach 1226, now with AEC A173 engine, was photographed in Bensham depot yard, these 1949 coaches were in their final season. They were, however, still smartly turned out for Day Tours in their final livery of cream and bus red, with 'curly' coach fleetname.

Among the single-deckers parked behind 1226 are 1947 Guy Arab/Brush 38-seater 1096, waiting for a Trading Estate (Team Valley) special, and 1940 AEC Regal/Picktree 38-seater 983, which would be one of the last prewar buses to be sold, in 1958. *Roy Marshall / Photobus*

▲ Before redevelopment of the Gateshead (ex-tram) depot, it was used for the storage of buses waiting for disposal. By October 1965 Guy Arabs and Leyland Titans were on the way out. The pick of the bunch was surely Gateshead 71, the penultimate PD2/1, which still looks fresh in chocolate with the non-Group-standard Newcastle Corporation blind box. The departure of the lightweight Orion-bodied Arabs was regretted by few, but the Weymann-bodied heavyweight Arab had provided comfortable but slow transport for 12 years, the fleet turnover period at the time. The Guys all went for scrap, but the 14-year-old PD2 turned up in Arbroath, Scotland, for further service with Greyhound. *R. L. Kell*

Any coaches which replaced the SE6s had a lot to live up to, and the 35-seat Guy Arab LUF 6HLW Continental tourers of 1954 suffered a little from the adoption of industry-standard 2+2 seating. No 1541 sparkles in the all-red mid-'Fifties coach livery, which was always well maintained, and the coaches were comfortable and well regarded. The chassis were delivered to Northern for modification, for example transferring the fuel filler to the UK nearside. The bodies were designed (by Doug Pargeter, ex-Northern Coachbuilders) and built at Picktree Coachworks at Chester-le-Street. The offside emergency exit was designed to allow regular use by passengers in Europe. The coach was posed at Team Valley by BET management trainee Tony Baker in 1957.
Roy Marshall / Photobus

In July 1975 the author found this 1955 Northern Guy Arab LUF running for Pritchard & Sons of Newborough, Anglesey. No 1665 was little changed from its time at Northern. This batch of 22 Weymann-bodied buses with Gardner 5HLW engines and five-speed gearboxes were quite speedy machines when wound up and saw early service on the Newcastle–Crook joint service (42) with United. The batch were later transferred to Winlaton depot. No 1665 was eventually bought by the North East Bus Preservation Society and is currently being renovated as the only remaining Northern Guy bus or coach.
R. L. Kell

▲ Newcastle Corporation owned Marlborough Crescent bus station, of which some of the exit stands are shown in 1957, when the roof was still in place. On the left, next to Northern's impressive booking/ enquiry office, is United Bay A, with a Bristol L5G about to depart on service 1 to Branch End via Ryton and Crawcrook, along the south bank of the Tyne. Northern Bays B and C play host to Saunders-Roe-bodied Leyland Tiger Cubs, one on the 43 to Kibblesworth and 1543 (the nearer) pulling out for Blaydon on service 9. In Northern's Bay D, AEC Reliance express coach 1714 waits to depart on one of the Company's original core services, the 2 to Stanley and Quaking Houses. On the right, in the shade, is a Willowbrook-bodied Atkinson of Venture Transport, Consett. *Roy Marshall / Photobus*

▲ Chester-le-Street's section of the former Great North Road was by-passed in the 1930s. Guy Arab IV 1637, with Metro-Cammell Orion body, was one of those without platform doors and by May 1968 was one of the last survivors of the 1955 batch. It has reached Chester via Wrekenton and will travel on to Houghton on the 75. The Arab/Orions provided noise and vibration in quantity but great reliability and economy. No 1637 still looks in good shape, but went for scrap the following year.

The Metro-Cammell body on AEC Reliance 1725 wasn't that comfortable either, particularly for the two-hour run from South Shields to Esh Winning — a service (62) taken over from the White & Nixon consortium in 1934. The all-red economy livery looked dismal on these 1950s standard single-deckers.

Wears shop in the background provided booking facilities for Northern's Coventry and Blackpool express services.
R. L. Kell

▲ The coach intake for 1956 consisted of 15 Weymann Fanfare 37-seaters. Ten were for Northern on Guy Arab LUF 6HLW chassis and five for Wakefield's on AEC Reliance. They always appeared in excellent condition and were re-trimmed and re-seated by Plaxton in 1964. They had long lives (for coaches) of 11 years or so. On a quiet Whitsuntide evening in 1963, Northern 1684 and 1686 and Wakefield's 198 are seen on a day tour on their final stop at Stokesley before return to Durham and Newcastle. In the background, a United Bristol MW service bus makes its way into the bus station. The Duple-bodied Bedford coach on the left is 3948 PT of Cleasby, Langley Moor, Durham.
R. L. Kell

The 15 Willowbrook-bodied AEC Reliances of 1956 (Nos 1710-24) represented a landmark in the fleet, being the first express or dual-purpose coaches. As such, they were in constant demand for express and trunk-service work, and their success in this role led to orders for many more.
No 1716, posed for the X62 Blackpool service, is seen in original condition in 1957.
Roy Marshall / Photobus

The five Albion Aberdonian MR11N chassis of 1957 had short lives, of 10 years.
The chassis was essentially an ultra-lightweight Leyland Tiger Cub and saved more than half a ton over the latter when fitted with similar 44-seat Weymann bodywork.
However, despite weighing barely 5 tons laden, the type was reckoned not to be over-endowed in the retardation department, and 1759, posed in original red and cream in 1957 for Stanley depot's workings on the Newcastle–Quaking Houses service, would later depart for the gentler gradients of Murton depot's services.
From 1958 NGT restricted the licensing of its fleet to County Durham (PT, UP) and Gateshead (CN), so the Aberdonians were its last new buses to bear the South Shields CU (Roman Caer Urfa ?) mark.
Roy Marshall / Photobus

The 20 NGT Titan PD3/4s of 1958 with Metro-Cammell bodies led quieter lives than did their Tynemouth/Wakefield's sisters. They were the first double-deckers delivered in the new 'all-red' (with cream band) livery and the last not to have platform doors. There was always a Sunderland contingent, originally for the longer services and latterly Sunderland locals, in this case to Red House Estate. Pictured in April 1970, 1844 is in the 'Tynemouth revival' livery resembling Northern's pre-1956 colours but without lining-out and black wings. The new fleetname has gone upstairs. Standing beside Binns' bakery in Park Lane are two AEC Reliances of the Anderson / Wilson Economic operations from Sunderland to South Shields via the coast road. They are Roe-bodied 2372 PT and, at the rear, UPT 630 with Duple body. *D. Little / Photobus*

▲ Northern's 10 PD2/12s of 1957 were ordered for Sunderland District but were needed to replace the 1955 Guy Arab/Orions on the longer joint (with United) services, particularly the Newcastle–Middlesbrough 55. They were notably speedy machines south of Durham, where the roads were more open. Only the cramped and none-too-comfortable seats let them down for longer-distance passengers. Later replaced by Atlanteans and Routemasters, the PD2s transferred to local services. Here 1764 is leaving Consett (and its Christmas illuminations) on snowy roads in January 1971, so the platform doors would have been appreciated. The ex-Witbank Durham 91 service was linked to the Consett–Castleside 20 service in 1970 as the 134.
D. Little / Photobus

The year 1958 marked a welcome change in specification for service buses, the large batch (34) of AEC Reliances with Burlingham 45-seat bodies having a higher standard of seat and internal trim, creating well-appointed and comfortable buses. They were delivered principally to Stanley and Consett depots to replace the 1939/40 AEC Regal 'utilities'. The bodies were not particularly robust and received attention in the Bensham body shops, most, like 1805, losing their decorative trim. The bus is working the Esh Winning–Newcastle (Marlborough Crescent) 54 service inherited from General County. In May 1968 a Northern inspector pays close attention to loading at the Newcastle stand; beside the shelter, a Northern poster-board advertises tours. Behind the Routemaster (bound for Worswick Street), the Chester Co-op dominates the street. *R. L. Kell*

The 20 Harrington Cavalier 37-seat coaches of 1960 (AEC Reliance) and 1961 (Leyland Leopard L2T — Northern's first Leopards) restored the coaching fleet to the highest standard, and the vehicles looked particularly well in the red-and-cream finish. Leopard 1959 was on a relatively mundane outing to Roker Park, Sunderland, on a football special in November 1962. After touring the Continent when new, the batch had long lives, of 14 years, which included express work, although some were fitted with bus seats after 10 years or so. The 'butterfly-grille' Bedford, UNE 56, was operating for Roberts of Wingate, Co Durham. *R. L. Kell*

The 20 AEC Reliances of 1961, with Alexander 41-seat dual-purpose bodies, were maids of all work on both bus and express work. From May 1968 six were hired to Tynemouth & District, No 1993, seen in Northumberland Square, North Shields, being allocated fleet number 310. They were transferred formally to the Tynemouth fleet in July 1969, 1993 as No 315. *Photobus*

The blinds on Routemaster
2101 cannot have been fully
re-set as the bus headed into
Newcastle across the Tyne
Bridge in May 1970.
The 85 was the Newcastle–
Washington Brady Square
service. The 50 Leyland-
engined Routemasters (plus
ex-LT RMF1254) were bought
for the longer inter-urban
services and thoroughly
justified their higher initial
cost, all having lives of 14 to
17 years in arduous service.

Behind the Routemaster,
AEC Reliance / Metro-Cammell
1730 comes in from Pelton
on the 7 service, followed by
a Newcastle Corporation
ETN-C Metro-Cammell-
bodied Leyland Atlantean,
with an older Northern Metro-
Cammell Atlantean behind.
R. L. Kell

▲ In March 1970 the author happened to be at Stanley when Northern's AEC Matador towed in 1963 AEC Reliance 2277, which had caught fire. Its BET-specification Willowbrook body had suffered severely, and the bus was duly written off. Oddly, no fewer than three of this batch of 19 suffered fire damage, 2270 being rebodied and returned to service but 2272 and 2277 ending their days early. Behind the Reliance stands AEC Monocoach 1622.
R. L. Kell

◄ Fifteen of these standard BET 53-seat buses by Marshall on AEC Reliance 2U3RA chassis were the sole single-deckers for 1964. All were in unrelieved red. No 2285 retains its original fleetname in capital letters on the side but has the new, lower-case design on the front. It is waiting to depart for Newcastle from Park Lane, Sunderland, but a semi-coach would be preferable for an X4 express.
Photobus

▲ In 1966 the coaching fleet added to stock 10 Leyland Leopards with Plaxton Panorama 44-seat bodies. Again, the disposition of the red and cream on one of the best Panorama variations produced a stunning result for these high-class tourers. No 2624 was brand-new when posed with Northern office staff and driver in 'appropriate surroundings' for publicity purposes. *Go North East*

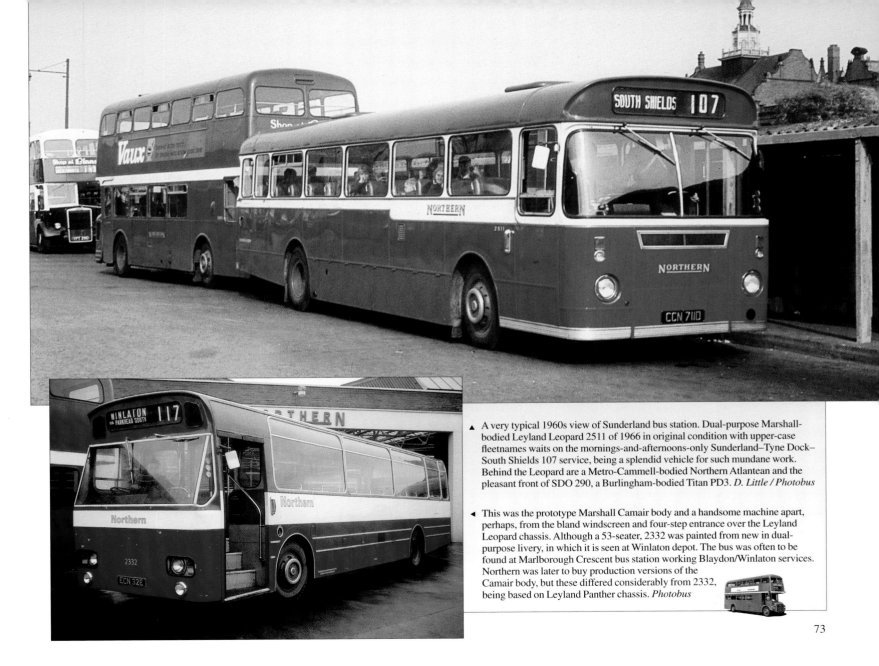

A very typical 1960s view of Sunderland bus station. Dual-purpose Marshall-bodied Leyland Leopard 2511 of 1966 in original condition with upper-case fleetnames waits on the mornings-and-afternoons-only Sunderland–Tyne Dock–South Shields 107 service, being a splendid vehicle for such mundane work. Behind the Leopard are a Metro-Cammell-bodied Northern Atlantean and the pleasant front of SDO 290, a Burlingham-bodied Titan PD3. *D. Little / Photobus*

This was the prototype Marshall Camair body and a handsome machine apart, perhaps, from the bland windscreen and four-step entrance over the Leyland Leopard chassis. Although a 53-seater, 2332 was painted from new in dual-purpose livery, in which it is seen at Winlaton depot. The bus was often to be found at Marlborough Crescent bus station working Blaydon/Winlaton services. Northern was later to buy production versions of the Camair body, but these differed considerably from 2332, being based on Leyland Panther chassis. *Photobus*

▲ A typical Northern line-up at Park Lane Garage, Sunderland.
From the left are Nos 1681 (Guy Arab LUF 6HLW / Weymann Fanfare
coach of 1955), 1958 (Leyland Leopard L2 / Harrington Cavalier coach
of 1961), 2148 (Leyland Atlantean / Alexander of 1967) and 2089
(AEC/Park Royal Routemaster of 1964). The 17 was a joint service
with Sunderland Corporation to Hylton Castle. *Photobus*

▲ The 12 Alexander-bodied Atlanteans of the XUP-F batch were the last double-deckers delivered under BET ownership. Their lives as 77-seaters with Northern were to prove very short, however, with their transfer to Gateshead in 1970 and conversion to dual entrance/exit for one-man operation. No 2164 is seen in September 1970, shortly before transfer, after unloading at Carliol Square. The 87 was an unusual service, travelling hourly to Jarrow and then around the southern outskirts of South Shields to end at the Marsden Inn, overlooking Marsden Rock on the coast (before it half-collapsed) and which was the southerly turning circle of the South Shields trolleybus system. Behind 2164, on the Darlington service, is 2184, one of the 1969 batch of Daimler Fleetlines sent to Maidstone & District in exchange for Fleetline single-deckers in 1972. *D. Little / Photobus*

▲ After the replacement of the Gateshead trams by buses in 1950, 19 of the characteristic long single-deck bogie cars were sold to the Grimsby & Immingham Electric Railway for further use, in British Railways green livery. After withdrawal in 1961, a couple were saved, and No 10 eventually ended up at Beamish North of England Open Air Museum, at Stanley, Co Durham. Restored to Gateshead livery, it is seen here in October 1973 at Beamish before the tram track was fully laid into the road surface. The tram, with body built at the Sunderland Road workshops in the 1920s, is now reckoned to have covered more miles at Beamish than in Gateshead service! *R. L. Kell*

The 7ft 6in-wide Leyland Titan PD2/1s of 1951 had a good innings at Gateshead. These three, Nos 62, 65 and 59, had just been withdrawn when photographed in October 1965, but all would see further service with Alexander of Arbroath in Scotland. The side view reveals the excellent draughtsmanship in the body profile of this classic double-decker. No 62 still retains its original black beading under the top-deck windows, and all the half-drop windows still fit squarely — quality indeed. No 65 still has its 'punched-hole' Leyland period wheeltrims. Vaux's beer lasted longer than the PD2, but regrettably the Sunderland brewery is now also but a memory. *R. L. Kell*

Gateshead's 1958 Metro-Cammell Orion-bodied Titan PD3s suited their original chocolate-and-cream livery particularly well. This depot view of February 1965 also shows a withdrawn Northern Guy Arab / Weymann in the background. The vans and van body belong to Hanson's of Huddersfield, which purchased the Gateshead Tramway Parcels Express business in April 1963 and still worked from the Sunderland Road depot, which was shortly to be redeveloped. *R. L. Kell*

The early batches of Gateshead Atlanteans were all delivered in traditional chocolate, but the cream was reduced to one band, and after a while they began to look dowdy, compared with Newcastle Corporation's bright cream and cadmium yellow. The 1960 and 1961 Atlanteans were bodied by Roe, and 104 of the second batch is seen at Barras Bridge, Newcastle, on the joint cross-Tyne North Kenton–Gateshead (Leam Lane Estate) service. The fawn-coated conductor is having a few moments' break from fare collection.
A. J. Douglas / Photobus

July 1967 and a busy scene on the Tyne Bridge, with plenty of 1950s and 1960s cars and three Alexander-bodied Leyland Atlanteans of Gateshead & District. This chassis/body combination was the most typical Tyneside bus, being used by all the Northern Group fleets and Newcastle Corporation. No 134 is working the Springwell–Newcastle–Fawdon service operated jointly with the Corporation. This 1965 bus was one of the second batch to be painted from new in the new livery of green and cream. The fourth Atlantean, heading out to Sunderland, is a Sunderland District Roe-bodied vehicle.
R. L. Kell

AEC Regents were always at home in the Tynemouth & District fleet from 1931 onwards, and the Weymann-bodied examples exemplified the fleet in the 1940s and 1950s. No 149 was one of the 1948 batch and is seen in North Shields in July 1958 in the 1956 'cream top' livery, introduced by James Forster, which eliminated black wings and lining-out — not the Tynemouth splendour your author remembers.

Family days out to Whitley Bay involved catching the bus to South Shields, crossing the Tyne on the smoky *Northumbrian* and rushing to get a seat on the Tynemouth or Wakefield's double-decker on the 8 service.

Climbing out of New Quay involved a sharp left turn on to the stiff Borough Road hill. Some drivers played it safe and used bottom gear and maximum revs the whole way up, the protesting Regent screaming as usual. More venturesome drivers snatched up into second and, with the bus leaning out round the corner, could get halfway up Borough Road. Then came the heart-stopping change into bottom on the steepest gradient, the Regent almost coming to a standstill. Would the driver make it? If not, it was downhill, backwards, into the river. They always did make it, of course. The Tynemouth trams had suffered a serious overturn when a tram 'got away' on a hill, and this lingered long in folk memory. *R. L. Kell*

▲ The Tynemouth/Wakefield's batch of 1958 Leyland
Titan PD3/4s with Metro-Cammell Orion bodies were
to a higher internal specification than the Northern
batch, but many ended up on loan to Northern (and
some other fleets) before being formally transferred.
Here, 230 is working for Northern at Chester-le-Street
depot in June 1968 and is ready to depart on a Lumley
local as a Routemaster pulls in front on a longer service.

Tynemouth pioneered the return to the traditional
red-and-cream livery in 1966, and its buses always had
a 'fresher' air about them than the all-red Northerns,
although some of the latter (including a few
Routemasters) were painted in the brighter colours.
No 230 still survives, with Trevor Hines of Sunderland.
R. L. Kell

After the 1962 Atlanteans, Tynemouth turned to the Daimler Fleetline for double-deckers, but the 1968 batch were the last (although the Group would later turn to the Fleetline single-decker in a big way) and the final deliveries under BET. Alexander-bodied 298 is seen in full Tynemouth livery in National Bus Company days (note that light-grey front wheel!) in South Shields in May 1973 on a bus service to Whitley Bay via the Tyne Tunnel, temporarily replacing the river ferry. *D. Little / Photobus*

Tynemouth's early rear-engined fleet mirrored Northern's, the first batch of such buses being nine Metro-Cammell Atlanteans, complete, as were Northern's, with 'Atlas' badges. Delivered in plain red (like 1895 on the cover), they were brightened up by Tynemouth's adoption of the old red and cream. No 237 is seen in the outskirts of Wallsend on a local service in March 1971. *D. Little / Photobus*

▲ The Alexander Y-type body was introduced to the Wakefield's fleet in 1968 by two 47-seat coaches on Leyland Leopard chassis. The coaches were painted, however, in dual-purpose livery. No 304 is seen on a Day Tour at Stokesley when quite new in August 1968. *R. L. Kell*

▲ In 1951, when still quite new, Northern 1389, a Leyland Titan PD2/3, was transferred to the Tyneside fleet (38), where it was identical to 'native' PD2s 34-7. Following withdrawal, it was sold in 1964 to Alexander of Arbroath, which took a number of Northern Group PD2s in the 1960s. Repainted red and cream (like its original NGT livery) it is seen in January 1966 near the Greyhound depot in Dundee. The route-number box had been overpainted at Tyneside, as numbers were not needed. *R. L. Kell*

The twin ventilation slots in the front dome gave the Tyneside PD2/12 / Orions a quizzical air and distinguished them from the other Group Orions. The batch of nine had route-number apertures, which were superfluous on the unnumbered Newcastle–Wallsend– North Shields (via Riverside) service. In this July 1966 view, at the new depot at Hadrian Road, Wallsend, 40 has lost its number section completely, giving it a lop-sided look; most were simply painted over. The hinged duplicate plate fitted to all Group half-cab double-deckers can be seen under the canopy. Although they seem in good condition, 39 and 40 would not last long, becoming the first Tyneside Orions to be withdrawn later in the year. *R. L. Kell*

Sunderland District's five Leyland Titan TD7s were praised for the way they performed on the Newcastle–Sunderland section of service 40, with a quiet gentle hum and splendid flywheel whine at high engine speed. On the right road, such as the easily graded A184, and with the best of coachwork, from Charles Roe of Leeds, they were unsurpassed until the PD2 came along. After 14 years of service, all five found buyers, and 173 was the best known, with Charlton-on-Otmoor Services in Oxfordshire. In May 1961 the bus was still in good shape in SDO blue, with light blue overpainting white. Beside it is a derelict ex-City of Oxford 1946 AEC Regent with Park Royal body. *R. L. Kell*

A good design looks well in most liveries, and the eight AEC Regent IIIs of 1950 with Roe coachwork were 'special'. After 12 years with SDO, the batch passed to Northern as 2042-9. The SDO single-line destinations were replaced by standard Northern displays with number boxes. Here Northern 2045, formerly SDO 227, leaves Newcastle on quiet roads for Chester-le-Street on a short working of the 46. In the background, another AEC Regent III, of Newcastle Corporation, enters the Tyne Bridge for Newcastle. It is one of the batch fitted with 8ft-wide Northern Coachbuilders bodywork derived from the contemporary Eastern Coach Works design. *R. L. Kell*

This July 1963 view captures SDO 233 in service with standard Northern blind boxes, having been withdrawn by SDO and sent to Bensham for conversion for Northern use, as 2074. Before repainting, an urgent need for buses to provide a service from Chester-le-Street to Durham County Show at Lambton Park meant that 233 was sent back to Philadelphia for the weekend; a few days later it was red. SDO PD2 / Orion 'bouncer' 275 in immaculate condition was next and a brand-new Northern Atlantean 2061 is third in line of stand-bys. The vehicles show '4', as the service was a short working of the Consett–Sunderland 4 service. *R. L. Kell*

Shortly before withdrawal, SDO Leyland Royal Tiger 253 was hired for an outing by the Northern Group Enthusiasts' Club. It ended up on a wet night in February 1966 at West Hartlepool — a place seldom reached by this batch — surrounded by United Bristol Lodekkas. The 1952 Royal Tigers were SDO's first 8ft-wide buses and real heavyweights (at 7 tons 14cwt) with very comfortable seating. These were the chassis that Major Hayter would not buy at Northern and the last buses to Mr Mountain's specification for SDO. *R. L. Kell*

The batch of 13 Titan PD3/4s with Burlingham bodies were perhaps SDO's best-known buses and were held in very high regard. With its 10 PD2 / Park Royal double-deckers ordered for 1957 having been diverted to Northern, and needing urgently to replace the inadequate Guy Arab / Orions on the long inter-urban services, SDO was in a pickle while waiting for the PD3s, and had to make do with various old Guy Arabs from Northern. The PD3s were worth waiting for, however, being better buses than the cramped PD2s, and were used all over the system. No 288, at Hetton-le-Hole in July 1966, wears its eight years of intensive service very well. Strangely, the number blind has not been set, but, unless a school or works special, the service must be a 49 from Newcastle via Sunderland. *R. L. Kell*

89

▲ SDO's first Atlanteans arrived in 1960 and, like Gateshead's first batch, had Alexander bodies which were not without teething troubles. In contrast to the PD2s and PD3s, they seemed a little unengaging — perhaps they were driven too well at SDO. This view, in April 1972, shows 305 in its last year with SDO, waiting to take up a football special to Roker Park in a curiously quiet Houghton-le-Spring Broadway. The parked cars behind it reveal that this is after the by-passing of Houghton by the new 'Cut' and the banishing of buses to a new bus station 15 minutes' walk from the shops, on the other side of the new A690. The predictable result of the removal of buses from the busy shopping streets of this local centre was the loss of local trade both to businesses and to bus travel. The new bus station was so unpopular that it became an 'enterprise centre' and the buses came back — but not until after damage to everyone except the motorist. *R. L. Kell*

▲ SDO 308 at the beginning of its life in Sunderland, in September 1960. The SDO livery adorns what turned out to be a none-too-satisfactory body by Charles Roe, SDO's traditional supplier. The steel frames of the early Northern Group Atlanteans corroded due to the local climate and the use of salt on winter roads. Rebuilding and recertification costs were high, although 308 would have a long life, passing to the Northern fleet in 1975. The 1956 Park Lane bus station can just be seen over the railway lines, now adapted as an interchange for the Tyne & Wear Metro extension to South Hylton. Behind 308, a Durham District Bristol L5G, JHN 362, transferred from the United fleet as DB276, waits to take up duty on the D3 service to Darlington. *R. L. Kell*

In 1960, supplementing 12 Atlanteans, Sunderland District bought a couple of Leyland Tiger Cubs to replace Tiger PS1 coaches sent to Northern. They were Metro-Cammell-bodied 43-seaters but, with high-back seats, were regarded as dual-purpose. In 1969 they were downgraded to one-man-operated buses, as can be seen from the front window notice in this July 1970 view of 312 at Chester-le-Street, waiting to depart on the 'back roads' 81 via Grasswell to Houghton-le-Spring. The extra beading confirms that it was originally light blue and cream. *D. Little / Photobus*

Two 1961 Tiger Cub / Burlingham coaches replaced the last of the Tiger PS1s at SDO. Originally used on Northern's seven-day tours, they were replaced on this work by the 1966 Plaxton Panorama-bodied Leyland Leopards. No 321, carrying miners in Dame Dorothy Street on a warm May day in 1972, will shortly turn left onto Monkwearmouth Bridge into Sunderland. The contraction of mining in central and west Durham left staff to be bussed to the collieries of east Durham, and Northern and SDO had considerable National Coal Board contracts in the 1960s and 1970s. Following NGT Routemaster 2093 has blinds reset for the return journey to Jarrow. *D. Little / Photobus*

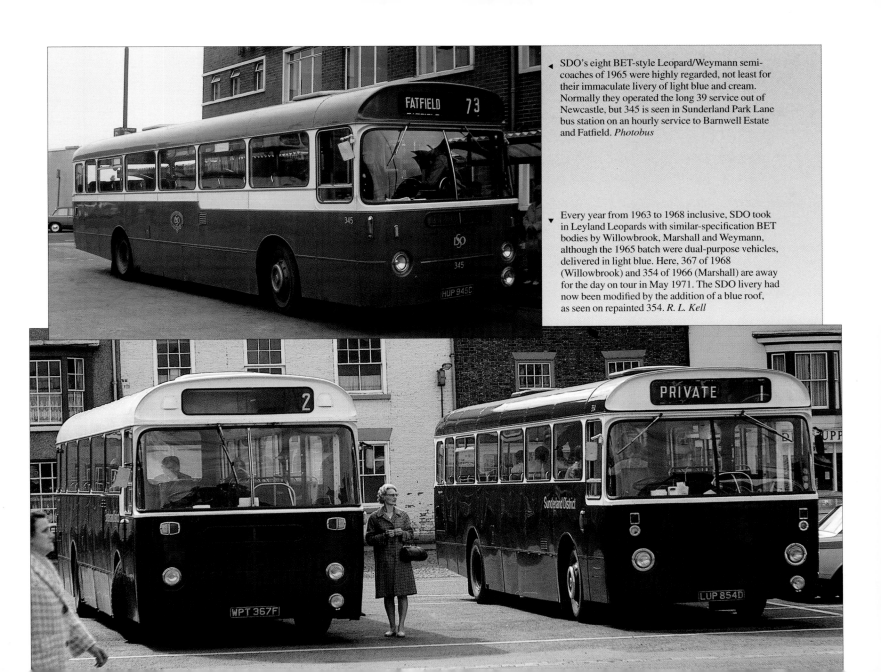

SDO's eight BET-style Leopard/Weymann semi-coaches of 1965 were highly regarded, not least for their immaculate livery of light blue and cream. Normally they operated the long 39 service out of Newcastle, but 345 is seen in Sunderland Park Lane bus station on an hourly service to Barnwell Estate and Fatfield. *Photobus*

Every year from 1963 to 1968 inclusive, SDO took in Leyland Leopards with similar-specification BET bodies by Willowbrook, Marshall and Weymann, although the 1965 batch were dual-purpose vehicles, delivered in light blue. Here, 367 of 1968 (Willowbrook) and 354 of 1966 (Marshall) are away for the day on tour in May 1971. The SDO livery had now been modified by the addition of a blue roof, as seen on repainted 354. *R. L. Kell*

Easington Lane had been the southerly terminus of the
Sunderland District Electric Tramways, and the trams used to
stand in the road to return north, next to where a red Northern
DP single-decker is waiting to set off for Newcastle on the
intensive and well-patronised 39 service (now 194/294).
Behind the unloading Mother's Pride bread van in June 1968
are two SDO Leopards, a 1965 Weymann-bodied DP in light
blue and cream and a 1968 Willowbrook-bodied bus.
More recently a turning-circle has been built behind the
War Memorial in the picture, so that buses terminating here
do not have to reverse on public roads. *R. L. Kell*

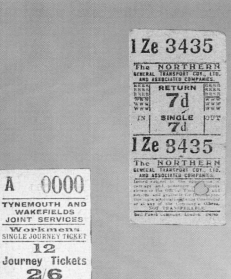

1 Ze 3435

The NORTHERN
GENERAL TRANSPORT COY., LTD.
AND ASSOCIATED COMPANIES.

RETURN
7d

IN **SINGLE** OUT
7d

1 Ze 3435

The NORTHERN
GENERAL TRANSPORT COY., LTD.
AND ASSOCIATED COMPANIES.

NOT TRANSFERABLE

Bell Punch Company, London.

K   9249

The Tyneside Tramways
and Tramroads Co. and
Newcastle Corporation
Transport Joint Service.

1 **3D** 4

SINGLE

2 5

Issued subject
to the Condi-
tions of Car-
riage and Pas-
senger Regula-
tions shown in
Official Time-
tables and
Notices.

3 6

NOT TRANSFERABLE.

Bell Punch Co. Ltd., London.

Ya   7099

SUNDERLAND DISTRICT
OMNIBUS COY., LTD.

RETURN
1/3

IN **SINGLE** OUT
1/3

Bell Punch Company, London.

Ya   7099

A   0000

TYNEMOUTH AND
WAKEFIELDS
JOINT SERVICES
Workmens
SINGLE JOURNEY TICKET

12
Journey Tickets
2/6

NOT TRANSFERABLE

Issued subject to
Conditions set out
on back cover.

12 Tickets 2/6

A   0000

To be retained by Conductor
Bell Punch Company, London.

Gr 06736

GATESHEAD OMNIBUS CO.

1d Issued subject to
Bye-laws and
Regulations.

ORD. CHILD WORKM.

HUNT. NOTTM.

LIMITED STOP
SERVICE. P

From DURHAM
To LEEDS
S FARE D

Voucher No.
45162

Class
£8

Date
5.10.56

SEE CONDITIONS ON BACK

G 835638

Bell Punch Company, Limited, London.

THE **NORTHERN**
GENERAL TRANSPORT COY., LTD. & ASSOCIATED COMPANIES

SHILLINGS	PENCE	STAGE IN
SINGLE		
RETURN		STAGE OUT

Issued subject to the Conditions of Carriage & Passenger Regulations shown in the Official Time-tables &
Notices, and available for free inspection upon application
to the Conductor or at any of the Company's Offices.

NOT TRANSFERABLE
Bell Punch Company, Limited, London.

569317 0

◄ NGT Group tickets: clockwise
from left are a Tynemouth/
Wakefield's Bell Punch
12-journey, Northern Bell
Punch, Tyneside Bell Punch,
SDO Bell Punch, 1950s Group
Bellgraphic and Limited Stop
(Newcastle–Liverpool)
Bellgraphic; in the centre is a
Gateshead 1d Ultimate.
R. L. Kell collection

NGT Chassis Production

Chassis No	Type	Date	Fleet Nos	Engine	Registration	Body
NGT1-63	Daim/NGT Y	1923-6	D113-258 range	P Daimler SV	PT, CN	B32F Brush, Vickers, RSJ
LY1-24	Daimler LY	1926	D268-91	P Daimler SV	PT, BR, CN	B32F BEF Brush, RSJ
LCB1-5	Daimler LCB	1926	D302-6	P Daimler SV	CN 2557-61	B32F BMMO Brush
64	NGT SE6	1933	586	P Hercules WXC2	CN 5674	B45F Short/NGT
65-9	NGT SE6	1934	604-8	P Hercules WXC2	CN 6100-4	B44F Short/NGT
70-5	NGT SE6/AEC	1935	657-62	P Hercules WXC2	CN 6616-21	B44F Short/NGT
76-80	NGT SE6/AEC	1935	T82/6/3-5	P Hercules WXC2	FT 3478/82/79-81	B44F Short/NGT
81-9	NGT SE6/AEC	1935	663-71	P Hercules WXC2	CN 6622-30	B44F Short/NGT
90	NGT SE6/AEC	1935	676	P Hercules WXC2	CN 6635	B44F Weymann/NGT
91-94	NGT SE6/AEC	1935	672-5	P Hercules WXC2	CN 6631-4	B44F Short/NGT
95-100	NGT SE6/AEC	1935	652/1/3-6	P Hercules WXC3	CN 6611/0/2-5	C28F Short/NGT
101	NGT SE4	1936	701	P Hercules WXC2	AUP 590	B40F EEC/NGT
102/3	NGT SE6	1936	727/8	P Hercules WXC3	CN 7430/1	C28F Beadle/NGT
104-6	NGT SE6	1936	T90-2	P Hercules WXC2	FT 3903-5	B44F Weymann/NGT
107-31	NGT SE4	1938/9	802-26	O AEC A172	CPT 902-26	B40F EEC/NGT
132	NGT/AEC	1951	1388	O AEC A173	BCN 888	FC35F Picktree A
133	NGT/AEC	1951	1402	O AEC A173	CCN 402	B43F Picktree/NGT
134-42	NGT/AEC	1952	1368-76	O AEC A173	CCN 368-76	FC35F Picktree A
143-48	Beadle/AEC (JCB252-7)	1952	W175-80	O AEC A173	FT 7275-80	FC35F Beadle
149	NGT/AEC	1952	1404	O AEC A173	CCN 404	FC35F Picktree A
150-9	NGT/AEC	1952	1457-66	O AEC A173	CCN 677-86	FC35F Picktree B
160-71	NGT/AEC	1953	1467-78	O AEC A173	DCN 67-78	B43F Picktree/NGT
172-4	NGT/AEC	1953	1493-5	O AEC A173	DCN 93-5	FC35F Picktree B
3000	Leyland/NGT	1972	3000	O Leyland O.600	MCN 30K	H39/29F MCW/NGT

Notes
Chassis 65-94, 101/4-6 to O AEC A172 or A183 1938 to 1946.
Chassis 65 to two-axle as LSE4 in 1941.
Chassis 70 to 100 assembled by AEC.
T: Tynemouth, W: Wakefield's
Chassis 65 and 3000 survive.
P: petrol, O: oil engine. SV: (Daimler) sleeve-valve.
Chassis 132/4-59/72-4 lengthened 1937 AEC Regal ('736' class).
Chassis 3000 constructed from Tyneside Leyland PD3 No 49 to normal-control, one-person layout.

Major Reconstructions

Early Daimlers rebuilt.

1932/3: seven Leyland Lion PLSC extended chassis, modified controls and short engine bay and new B38F Short bodies to NGT design.

1933: two SOS QC, 1925, fitted with new lengthened chassis and new B36F Short bodies designed by NGT.

The 1938/9 AEC Regal B and their 1949/50 rebodying, the 1947-50 Guy Arab single-deckers and the 1954 Guy Arab LUF coaches were all regarded as NGT 'special vehicles'.

To this may be added the 1946 reconstruction of SOS IM6 and ON to oil engines.